Thinking about fostering?

A practical guide

Emma Harding

Please note: All the foster carers mentioned in the book gave permission for their stories to be told. However, to protect their identity and the identities of the children they care for, all names and any personal details have been changed.

For Dad

Contents

Acknowledgements

Firstly my thanks to all the amazing foster carers I have met or spoken to over the years, particularly the ones I interviewed for inclusion here. You do the most fantastic job and are the inspiration for this book.

I am also grateful for the support of a number of fostering agencies, including Enfield Council, Isle of Anglesey Council, Northumberland Council and Park Foster Care. I'd also like to thank all the fostering agencies I've worked with over the last 15 years especially the team at Cheshire West and Chester Council.

Thanks also to Lesley Goode for allowing me to tap into her expertise and experience, Alison Jones and Jessica Peel-Yates for providing exactly the sort of detailed, insightful advice I needed and my sister, Kate Furniss, for her invaluable feedback on the book.

Then there are those who have cheered me on over the months and, in doing so, helped the book to fruition. These include Rebecca Stevens, Heather Pritchett, Suzanne Hudson, Andrew Shephard and Virginia Hainsworth. My apologies to anybody I have left out.

And finally, it almost goes without saying, but not quite - thanks and much love to my mum and to AB.

Introduction

Imagine one day far in the future. You're thinking about the children you have fostered over the years. Perhaps you looked after one child. Perhaps many.

You've had your fair share of difficulties and times when you seriously considered throwing in the towel. But you didn't. You gritted your teeth and got on with it. Because you knew they needed you to.

And it was worth it. You remember the little girl who didn't say a word until you made gingerbread together and her smile lit up the room. Or the boy, who had never used a knife and fork before, wolfing down fish fingers. Or the child who, after you'd helped him learn to cycle, said, "each time I ride my bike I'll think of everything you've done for me."

As a foster carer, you've come to realise that whatever you've had to deal with and whatever the outcome, you have made a real difference to the life of each and every child you've cared for. That's why you foster.

So will that be you in a few years' time? Are you thinking about changing your life and the lives of vulnerable children? Are you thinking about becoming a foster carer? If so, then this is the book for you. It will help you understand exactly what fostering is, who it helps and what sort of person makes a good foster carer. Hopefully it will help you to decide that fostering is something you could do and guide you on the first steps to becoming a foster carer.

First of all, some facts

On any one day, over 63,000 children are in foster care in the UK. Foster care provides them with a safe, secure and nurturing home for as long as they need it, whether that's a few days, a few months or for the rest of their childhood. Foster carers look after these children in the carers' own homes to give them as normal a life as possible.

The foster care system is overseen by the UK Government and managed by local councils in England, Wales and Scotland and by health & social care trusts in Northern Ireland.

Children of all ages, from babies to teenagers, need foster care. Foster carers might help brothers and sisters to stay together or children with disabilities to get the support they need.

Sadly, many of the children who need foster care have

experienced some form of neglect, abuse or trauma. Foster carers play a vital role in giving them the positive experiences they might have missed out on, helping them to grow in confidence and develop the skills that they'll need in the future.

Not enough foster carers

Unfortunately, in the UK, there is currently a shortfall of around 8,500 foster carers a year. Not having enough suitable foster homes can result in children being placed a long way from their families, friends and school. Sometimes it means that a child is moved around a lot when what they really need is a long-term and stable place to stay. This, of course, can be highly stressful for them and make it difficult for them to settle and build trusting relationships.

People who foster

All sorts of people become foster carers. Fostering agencies welcome people with a wide range of experience and from diverse backgrounds so that they can support the varying and complex needs of different children and teenagers. You can foster whether you're single, married, divorced, co-habiting, gay or lesbian – as long as you have the skills and qualities to help vulnerable children.

This book will cover what those skills and qualities are and what practical arrangements you need to have in place in order to foster. It will also look at how you go about becoming a foster carer, taking you step-by-step through the process so that you know what to expect.

The role of the foster carer

The foster carer's main task is to give a child a place to stay and as normal a life as possible. But there's much more to it than that. A foster carer helps the child in their care to keep in contact with their own family, if this is appropriate for them, as well as working as part of the team responsible for making sure the child gets all the help they need.

Foster carers receive an allowance to cover the costs of caring for a child or children. Some fostering agencies also pay foster carers a fee. In most cases these allowances and fees are only paid when a foster carer has a child living with them.

Foster carers' stories

One of the best ways to find out more about fostering is to talk to foster carers themselves. They can give you the lowdown on the realities of fostering, the challenges they've faced and how they dealt with them and, importantly, the many rewards that come from helping a child who's going through a really difficult time. This book features the real-life stories of several foster carers who share their thoughts about fostering, including why they decided to foster and how they've helped the children in their care.

A big decision

Fostering is a really important role and an immensely rewarding one. It is however a very challenging one too. It is vital that anyone considering fostering goes into it with their eyes open. If you've got lots of questions, lots of uncertainties, even lots of worries about fostering that's a good thing. It means you understand it's not something to be taken lightly. It means you'll work hard to discover the facts. It also means you're in the right place. This book will answer many of your questions, address those uncertainties and reassure you about some of your worries. By providing lots of useful information and dispelling many of the myths about fostering, this book will help you decide whether becoming a foster carer is the right decision for you and your family.

1. What is fostering?

Think about a child you know. Perhaps your own son or daughter or a grandchild, a niece or nephew. Maybe the child of a friend. Imagine they can't live at home for some reason and there's no one amongst family or friends who can look after them.

Where will they live? Who will look after them? How will they be treated? How will they feel?

It's unsettling, isn't it, to contemplate any child we know being in this situation? We worry about how upset they would be, being separated from their family, how confused and anxious it might make them. We want them to be protected from harm. Most of all, we hope that they are living with caring, sensitive people who will support them through this difficult time, help them to enjoy life and reassure them about what's happening.

In other words, we hope they're in the care of really

good foster carers.

You may or may not already know a child who's in this situation. But every day around 63,000 children in the UK are living with foster carers (ref: Fostering Network). They need the same things your imagined child does – a safe place to live, care, attention, reassurance, consistency and stability. And that is what foster care provides.

This chapter addresses in detail what fostering actually is, the organisations that are involved in making sure vulnerable children get the care they need and the role of the foster carer.

The definition of fostering

Sometimes it is not possible or safe for a child to live with their own parents or family. This can be for many different reasons. In these circumstances, a child might be 'taken into care' by their local council and an alternative place for them to stay will be sought. One which will keep them safe from harm and provide the care and support that they need.

Foster care is one such alternative. A foster carer looks after a child in the carer's own home, meeting the child's day-to-day needs. In most cases this is a full-time commitment – the child will live with the foster carer 24/7 - but the length of their stay (known as a placement) will depend on what's happening with their own family and what's best for them. It could be for a few days, months or years.

Fostering is a job. Foster carers are paid for the work they do and will also receive money to cover the cost of looking after a child or children, such as buying food, clothes or toys. They will also receive support and training. They will work together with social workers and other professionals to make sure the child gets the support they need.

Most foster carers find that fostering is a very satisfying thing to do. They make a real and crucial difference to a child, supporting them through a difficult period in their lives.

The difference between fostering and adoption

Adoption is another alternative for a child who cannot live with their own family. However, unlike foster care, it is a permanent arrangement whereby the adoptive parents become the legal guardians of the child through a formal court process.

Foster carers are not the legal guardians of the child, however long the child remains in their care. It is the local council that is ultimately responsible for the care of the child. Foster carers provide the temporary care that a child needs while the situation with their own family is resolved or before they are moved on to a permanent arrangement like adoption.

As we will see later, there is such a thing as long-term fostering, when a child will live with foster carers until they reach 18. This is because it is not appropriate for them ever to return home to their family but adoption is not the right solution for them. This might be because they need to maintain a relationship with their own parents that would not be possible if they were adopted. If appropriate, foster carers can apply for a special guardianship order (SGO) which gives them parental responsibility for the child until they're 18.

Residential care

The other potential alternative for children 'in care' is to live in residential care, i.e. children's homes. These are very different from the orphanages and institutions of the past – often small units of just a few children and residential workers. While foster care is usually preferred over residential care, sometimes children find it really hard to be in a family environment and can benefit from a different set-up that is perhaps less intense. Sometimes children are placed in residential care because their behaviour cannot be dealt with in a family setting.

As you can see, there are several options when it comes to where a child lives if they cannot live with their own family, whether that's short-term or long-term foster care, adoption or residential care. The important thing is that the decision about which of the options is selected is made in the best interests of the child.

The organisations involved in foster care

It is a sad fact that, for some children, living with their own families is not in their best interests. They may be at risk of serious harm. In order to protect them, it might be that the only option is to remove these children from their homes and place them where they will be safe and well looked after. Removing children who are at risk from harm is called child protection.

Given the complexity and sensitivity surrounding the removal of children from their families, it is vital that the people making these decisions and providing that care are properly managed and regulated. That's why there are a number of public and private sector organisations involved in child protection and the provision of foster care.

The Government

The role of the Government (whether in England, Wales, Scotland or Northern Ireland) is to establish legislation and regulations about:

• how vulnerable children are protected and looked after

• the role of foster carers

• how foster carers should be assessed and supported.

All fostering agencies are regulated by the respective country's government and are regularly inspected to ensure they are performing to the appropriate standards. You can read the inspection report for any agency (see Helpful Resources for details).

The Government has established a series of national minimum standards for foster care which outline the fundamental elements of care that a foster carer should provide. You can find these standards by visiting www.gov.uk and searching for 'fostering minimum standards.'

Legislation differs across England, Wales, Scotland and Northern Ireland. Check out Helpful Resources for how to find the relevant legislation for each country.

Local councils

In England, Scotland and Wales, local councils are responsible for all the children who have been 'taken into care' (i.e. removed from their family for their own protection) in their local area. In Northern Ireland it is the health and social care (HSC) trusts that have this responsibility.

The local council/HSC trust must decide the best course of action for each child (sometimes referred to as Looked After Children) including where they should live, who should look after them and under what circumstances they might be able to return to their parents. This is known as a care plan. A team of people is involved in developing and implementing this plan, including the child's foster carers.

Each child will have their own social worker, responsible for making sure that the child is getting the support they need. They are also likely to be working with the child's family to try and address the issues that are preventing the child from living at home.

Each local council/HSC trust will have a fostering service as part of its children's services or social work department which will manage a cohort of foster carers that it has recruited from the local area. It is responsible for assessing, training, paying and supporting these carers.

Independent fostering providers (IFPs)

Independent fostering providers are private or voluntary organisations that recruit, assess, pay and support foster carers. They may operate locally, regionally or nationally. For instance well-known children's charities Barnardo's and Action for Children also operate as independent fostering providers.

While the responsibility for planning and monitoring how each child in care is looked after remains with the local council, independent fostering providers are responsible for the foster carers they have recruited and the children those foster carers look after. Their role is to make sure their foster carers are suitably trained and supported to look after children properly.

If a local council is unable to place a child within its own group of foster carers it will sub-contract to an independent fostering provider to supply suitable foster carers to look after that child.

Foster carers perform the same role whether for the local council or an independent fostering provider. It is up to you to decide which you would prefer to work for. You'll find more detail about this in chapter seven.

In this book the term 'fostering agency / agencies' is used to refer to both local council/trust fostering services and independent fostering providers.

The Fostering Network

The Fostering Network is the UK's leading charity for everyone involved in fostering. Its work includes campaigning to improve policy, advising Government, raising awareness amongst the public about fostering and the need for foster carers and providing support and resources for foster carers and fostering agencies.

British Association of Adoption and Fostering (BAAF)

BAAF is a national adoption and fostering membership association. It works to promote high standards in adoption, fostering and childcare services. One of its aims is to raise understanding amongst the public of the issues surrounding fostering and adoption and has a huge range of publications and leaflets with more information about all aspects of foster care.

There are many other organisations involved in foster care, providing support and guidance to foster carers. You'll find some of these listed in the Helpful Resources section at the end of the book.

The role of the foster carer

In many ways you look after a foster child in the same way you would look after your own child. Foster carers make sure that children in their care have regular and healthy meals, that they get plenty of fresh air and exercise, that they go to school and do their homework and get to bed at a reasonable time. They make sure that there are lots of opportunities to have fun too, by taking them to new places, going to the park for a play on the swings or a kick-about, teaching them to ride a bicycle, helping them learn to swim, reading them a bedtime story, going to the cinema, playing video games, having their friends round for tea. Of course, they provide lots of support and encouragement too by listening to the child's troubles, offering advice on how to deal with difficult or new situations and praising them when they do well.

Caring for a troubled child

That all sounds like normal family life, doesn't it? But many children who need foster care won't have experienced a normal family life. Their childhood up to this point may well have been pretty traumatic. They might have been neglected or abused. Life might have been very chaotic or even frightening. This is why foster care is so important. For many foster carers the fact that children in care haven't had the sort of upbringing that other children have is the very reason they foster – to give these children the chance to experience what most children take for granted.

But it is also the reason why fostering is more than simply looking after a child. It is often about looking after a troubled child. A child who might be angry, confused, afraid, lonely, anxious or traumatised. They might lack basic skills, like eating with a knife and fork. They might find it difficult to trust you or to communicate how they feel. They might express their anger or anxiety by withdrawing into themselves or through bad behaviour.

So the role of the foster carer is also to support them and help them to deal with their experiences, to build trust, increase their self-esteem and show them how to behave appropriately.

This will take a lot of resilience, patience and time. It can be the most challenging aspect of foster care, but is often the most rewarding too. Foster carers frequently talk about the joy of watching a child blossom as a result of that patience and care.

Foster carers may also need to help the child maintain a relationship with their own family whether that's through face-to-face meetings or via letters, emails or telephone calls.

There's much more detail on the foster carer's role in chapter eleven.

Working as part of a team

It's important to remember that foster carers do not work in isolation. They are part of a team of professionals that will include social workers and may also include health workers, psychologists and teachers. This team works together to determine the sort of care and support the child needs now and to plan for their care in the future.

Foster carers receive training both before they become

foster carers and while they are looking after children. Each foster carer or couple will have their own social worker who visits regularly and provides advice and support on all aspects of foster care. It is also this social worker's job to check that the foster carers are providing a good standard of care and that any problems or issues are dealt with promptly and effectively.

Remember:

- Over 63,000 children are living with foster carers on any one day in the UK.

- Foster carers provide a safe place to live for children who have been taken into care by the local council because they cannot live at home.

- Unlike adoptive parents, foster carers are not the legal guardians of the child. This responsibility remains with the local council while the child is in care.

- The Government regulates and inspects all fostering agencies to ensure they meet legislative standards of care. Legislation varies across the UK.

- Local councils are responsible for all the children 'in care' in their area. Each child will have a care plan which outlines how they will be looked after and for how long.

- Foster carers can either work for their local council or an independent fostering provider.

- Foster care is about more than looking after the day-to-day needs of a child. It's often about helping a troubled child who may have been abused or neglected in some way.

2. Why are foster carers needed?

Foster care plays a vital role in society by protecting and caring for those children who cannot, for whatever reason, be looked after by their own families.

This chapter looks briefly at how and why foster care as we know it today developed. We'll see why some children can't live with their own parents and how foster care benefits them. We'll also see why there is a shortfall in the number of foster carers currently and the impact this has on vulnerable children.

A brief history of foster care

There is a traditional African saying that it takes a village to raise a child. It is possible that this idea lies at the root of the origins of foster care many hundreds of years ago - in the informal arrangements made between families and within communities to share the care of children.

Care in large institutions, such as residential schools and orphanages, also has a long history, going back as far as the Middle Ages.

In the late nineteenth and early twentieth centuries, most 'substitute' care (i.e. by adults other than the child's parents) of children took place in residential institutions, often run by charitable organisations. Thomas Barnardo opened his first children's home in 1870 for destitute children and orphans. He also established some of the first fostering schemes by 'boarding out' vulnerable children with alternative families.

Following the Second World War, during which many children were evacuated from cities to live with families in the country, the Children Act 1948 made foster care the preferred form of substitute child care. It also increased the amount of supervision children and their foster carers received. Regulations introduced in 1955 set out how these arrangements should be monitored and assessed.

Since then legislation has continued to develop in this area. In 1989 a new Children Act put the welfare of the child at the centre of any arrangements made for them and set out that the duty of the local council towards children in its care was to 'safeguard and promote their welfare.'

The impact of high profile child abuse cases

Two high profile cases of child deaths - Victoria Climbié who died in 2000 after abuse and neglect at the hands of her great-aunt and her boyfriend, and Baby P who died in 2007 after sustaining over 50 injuries inflicted by his mother and her two male friends - led to widespread public condemnation of those organisations that had failed to intervene.

Subsequent legislation has attempted to improve the way in which those agencies involved in child protection work together to identify and address cases of abuse and neglect.

These cases and others since have contributed to a 12% increase in the number of children taken into care between 2009 and 2013 (ref: Department of Education).

Why some children need foster care

Children come into the care system for many different reasons. For some it is because their parent/parents are unable to look after them due to illness or disability. Some families request that their child is taken into care because they can't cope with the child's behaviour or disability. However, this is relatively rare. One of the main reasons why children need foster care is because they are at risk from harm at home. They may have been neglected or experienced some form of abuse, be that emotional, physical or sexual. It is estimated that about 60% of children who come into the care system have been abused or neglected (ref: Department of Education).

Neglect is defined as a failure to meet a child's basic physical, psychological and/or emotional needs. It might involve a lack of adequate food, clothing or shelter, a failure to protect the child from harm or to ensure they get the medical care they need.

Emotional abuse is described as the persistent emotional mistreatment of a child. It might include giving the child the impression that they are worthless or unloved. It might involve preventing them from joining in with normal activities. It might involve them having to witness the abuse or bullying of another person in their household.

The impact of emotional abuse or neglect

Most of us can understand how much damage is done by physical neglect (malnutrition for instance) or physical abuse. But until recently there's been less awareness of the devastating effects of emotional neglect and abuse. However, research has been conducted in this area over the last ten years which has shown how a child's development is dramatically affected by the way in which they are cared for (this is often referred to as 'attachment theory').

From the minute it is born, a baby is programmed to form an attachment with their closest carer. A parent or carer who is loving, available, consistent, warm and attentive provides what's known as a secure base, the firm foundations and attachment a child needs in order to develop emotionally. Having a secure base helps build self-esteem and emotional resilience and will enable the child to form healthy bonds with other people.

If a parent or carer is very inconsistent with their love and attention or is rejecting, distant, unpredictable or aggressive, this can make the child feel insecure. This sense of insecurity can have a major impact on their development. They will find it hard to form a healthy attachment to their parent or carer and they may find it difficult to trust others to look after them. Their own sense of self-worth will be affected. Studies have shown that the areas of the brain that respond to stress develop abnormally in a child who is abused which can lead to long-term psychological and emotional problems.

This sort of abuse can affect all areas of a child's development – from speech and language to being able to make friends and progress at school. Children may develop problems dealing with emotions like fear and anger and may be prone to anxiety and depression. As teenagers and young adults they are more likely to fall into delinquency, criminal behaviour and drug addiction. It may also affect how they bring up their own children.

Attachment theory research has shown how experiences of poor care in early childhood result in what's known as 'attachment disorders' – a range of behaviours and emotional responses that are a child's way of expressing and dealing with the impact of this abuse. You'll find more detail about this in chapter eleven.

How foster care helps children

Foster care is obviously not a magic wand that can solve all the complex issues involved in a child being taken into care nor banish the harmful effects of a child's early experiences.

However, research does show that the negative impact of poor care in early childhood need not be permanent. Early intervention and significant improvement in how the child is cared for – whether by the parents themselves or by foster carers or adoptive parents – can help to minimise the damage.

Foster care benefits children in a number of ways:

I. By supporting their well-being

One of the main reasons a child who has experienced some form of abuse might be placed with foster carers is to protect them from harm. Foster care means they have a safe place to stay.

Foster care also provides the basic things that are so essential to a child's general well-being but which may have been missing from their childhood. Things like healthy and regular meals, shelter, clothing and warmth plus health care and exercise.

Foster care can also improve the child's emotional well-being by providing the support and comfort they need to help them to build trust, self-esteem and resilience.

This can also help the child's development, in terms of speech and language, doing well at school, learning new skills and making friends.

2. By giving them a sense of stability and security

As we have seen, children can become insecure if they

do not receive consistent care that responds quickly and appropriately to their needs. Foster care helps to counter that by providing them with the attention, support and stability that they need. Having reliable access to attentive and sensitive carers will help the child start to trust that they will be looked after.

3. By helping them deal with their emotions

Many children who have experienced neglect, abuse or trauma can find it difficult to manage their emotions. Their feelings of anxiety, anger and confusion are often expressed instead through challenging behaviour or highly emotional reactions to situations they find upsetting.

Foster care provides a supportive environment where children can learn to express their feelings more constructively.

Why more foster carers are needed

Since the tragic cases of Victoria Climbié and Baby P, and research into the effects of emotional abuse, there has been an increased focus on child protection. This has led to an increase in the number of children coming into care.

Which means, inevitably, there is a need for more foster carers. The Fostering Network estimates that around 8,500 more carers are required each year.

Without more foster carers being recruited across the UK, children may have to be placed further away from family, friends and their school than is desirable. This may in turn lead to more disruption and stress for them. They may have to go to a new school. It may be difficult for them to maintain a relationship with their own family. A lack of suitable foster carers also means that children may face having to move through a series of temporary homes rather than finding the long-term solution that would really benefit them.

More foster carers mean that children can be better matched with carers in their locality who can best meet their needs.

Remember:

- Foster care has a long history, but became more formal and regulated after the Second World War.

- High profile cases have increased public awareness of child abuse and led to increased scrutiny of those organisations charged with protecting children from harm.

- Since the Baby P case, the numbers of children being taken into care has increased dramatically.

- Recent research has shown how neglect and emotional abuse can be as damaging as physical abuse and impacts on a child's psychological and emotional development.

- A lack of consistent, loving care in early childhood can lead to feelings of insecurity, anxiety and confusion.

- Foster carers help child in their care by providing the stability, support and attention the child may have missed out on.

- According to the Fostering Network (2015), 8,500 more foster carers are needed each year to ensure children can benefit from the stability of high quality foster care.

3. Could you foster?

There are lots of misconceptions about who can and can't foster. People discount themselves from becoming foster carers because they're single or rent their home or work full-time. This chapter gives you the facts so that you can assess whether fostering's something you could do.

Who can and can't foster

There is no blueprint for the perfect foster carer. In fact it's really important that foster carers come from diverse backgrounds with different life experiences and skills. That way, they're better able to meet the diverse needs of the children in care. What they do share are a range of skills and qualities which enable them to provide vulnerable children with the care they need. We'll get to these a little later in this chapter.

So you can foster if you can see yourself in this list:

- You're married, in a civil partnership or co-habiting and the relationship is stable

- You're single and have a good support network around you

- You're gay, straight, bisexual or transsexual

- You have a disability or medical condition that doesn't impair your ability to care for a child

- You've children of your own or you've never had any children

- You own your home or you rent and have a stable tenancy

- You work full-time, part-time, are unemployed, self-employed or retired

- You're from any ethnic group – foster carers from all different cultures are needed so that children can be matched with suitable families.

You can't foster if you have a police record for violence or offences against children.

Some basic criteria

So, as you can see, there are very few factors that would automatically disqualify you from fostering. However, that doesn't mean, of course, that everyone can foster. You need to be able to fulfil some specific criteria in order to perform this role successfully:

For instance, it's essential that:

- You have room in your home and in your life to care for a child or children

- You are willing to work with the other people in the child's life – such as their family, social workers and other professionals

- You can understand or are prepared to learn, how children behave when they've been emotionally or physically hurt

- You're willing to attend training courses and support groups

- You have some experience of caring for other people, such as raising your own children, or working with children or vulnerable adults

- You have a healthy lifestyle (for instance children under five will not be placed with people who smoke)

- You, or your partner, are available to look after a child before and after school, during holidays and when the child is sick.

The skills you need

It is worth thinking carefully about what you would bring to foster care – and if you think you have the skills to do it well. Here are some of the skills, attributes and abilities that you will need:

Patience and empathy – foster children have, typically, been through a lot and this can often result in some quite challenging behaviour. You'll need to be patient, to recognise what's causing that behaviour, while setting boundaries and helping them to improve the way they behave. This could mean helping them to understand their own behaviour and providing guidance on how they should deal with difficult situations and emotions.

Commitment and resilience – foster children may have moved around a lot which can make it difficult for them to settle and to form bonds with the people looking after them. It may take time for them to learn to trust you so you'll need to commit to the long haul. It takes real commitment to work through the challenging times and offer the children in your care the reassurance of a secure and stable home environment.

A positive approach – you'll need to be able to work through any problems in a positive way and help the child to do so too. It's really important that you give the child lots of good experiences too.

A realistic outlook – often foster care is about taking small steps with the child and recognising even their smallest achievements. You'll need to be realistic about what you can do to help the child and also about what the child is able to achieve.

A professional approach – it's important to recognise that fostering is a job and requires a professional attitude. You will be expected to keep a record of the child's behaviour and development, and contribute to discussions about the child's care plans and their future.

Tolerance – children come from a range of backgrounds so it's vital that you are tolerant of different views, religious beliefs, life choices and sexuality etc.

Flexibility – foster carers need to be able to quickly adapt to changing circumstances. It might be for instance, that you need to respond to a change in arrangements for the child to see their own family. Or to be able to get up to speed quickly with the needs of a child who has just arrived.

Confidence – it's also important that you are confident enough to stick up for the needs of the child. Are they getting the support they need from the local council or their school for instance? Part of your role is to be the child's advocate.

Organised – there's a fair amount of paperwork to keep on top of so being well-organised is a key skill. You'll also need to attend appointments and meetings so good diary management and time-keeping skills are a must.

Practical essentials – what you'll need

It's not just your personal qualities that are important. A child will be coming to live with you so it's also vital that your home environment is suitable. The first and most critical thing is that you have a spare room in your house so that a foster child will have their own bedroom. Most fostering agencies will only consider your application if you have a spare room. Other than that there are no hard and fast rules about your home. Clearly it needs to be a safe and healthy environment and some outside space is preferable. It doesn't matter if you have pets as long as they don't pose any sort of danger to a child. Essentially your home needs to be child-friendly – things like open stairs or a garden pond might be a problem although clearly this will depend on the age or physical ability of the child who might be living with you.

Other practical considerations include whether you can drive and have access to a car. Part of your role will be to take the child to appointments so being able to drive is important unless you live in an area where you have access to good reliable public transport.

You'll also need to consider whether you have the time to look after a child. While many foster carers also work full-time, some fostering agencies prefer at least one foster carer to be at home during the day to be able to provide constant care. If you have very young children of your own, under two years of age, it is likely that a fostering agency would suggest you wait until your children are older before applying to become a foster carer.

Involving the rest of your family

If you are fostering as a couple then it's vital that you both meet the criteria outlined above and that you're both equally committed to foster care.

If you have children of your own who live with you, it is

important to think through and discuss how they might be affected by you becoming a foster carer. In reality, it's the whole family who fosters not just the adults. Many foster carers' children benefit from sharing their home with a foster child. They might form long-lasting friendships or develop important skills. But they might also find it disruptive or resent not having your full attention. You'll need to make sure, before applying to become a foster carer, that everyone in your family, including your own children, is onboard. It's worth knowing that many fostering agencies provide support for the children of foster carers, so check to make sure the one you apply to is one of them.

It's also a good idea to involve your wider family and your friends. There will be periods of stress and frustration and you'll need to have people you can turn to who can provide support when you need it, whether that's a sympathetic ear when you need to let off steam or more practical support, like babysitting. This sort of support network is particularly important if you are fostering as a single person.

Fostering or adoption?

It's worth thinking carefully about your motivations to foster. What's driving this interest? What can you offer a child? In what way do you want to help children? If your desire is to offer a permanent family home to a child or children then adoption might be more appropriate for you than fostering (although there is a type of fostering that means you care for a child until they reach adulthood). If you want to help as many children as possible and are prepared to look after a series of children then fostering is likely to be where your heart lies. There's no harm in exploring both options at this stage but it's important to recognise that they are very different in terms of your role. The assessment process (see chapter nine) and the criteria for who can adopt is, though, very similar to fostering.

Remember:

- There is no one type of person who makes a good foster carer. They come from all sorts of different backgrounds but they do share certain skills and qualities.

- You can foster whether you're married, co-habiting or single, whether you own your home or rent, whether you're disabled or not, whether you work full-time, part-time or are unemployed or retired.

- You'll need certain skills and qualities, like patience, commitment, tolerance and a professional approach.

- You'll need a spare room so the foster child can have their own bedroom and your home needs to be child-friendly.

- You'll need to have time in your life to care for a child.

- Remember that all your family will be involved in foster care so consider how it might impact on them.

- Consider what support you have available to you – your wider family, close friends etc who will be there for you when you need them to be.

4. June's story

"I do it because this is my calling."

June is 43 and married to Peter. They have five children and seven grandchildren. They live in north Wales.

June and Peter have been fostering for two and half years for their local council. They are approved to look after two children aged from 0 and 9 and to provide respite, short term and emergency foster care.

They have two foster children currently living with them, a boy of four who has been with them for nearly two years and a five year old girl who's been with them for almost a year.

I wanted to foster from an early age

June grew up in South Africa. She has a clear memory of being about 10 and being asked what she wanted to do when she grew up. "*I said, 'I want to be a mum and look after all the children who can't be looked after at home.' For that I got rapped across the knuckles with a ruler and told not to be stupid. The teacher said 'that's not a job, that's what women do anyway.' But I said, 'I want to look after the children who can't stay in their own homes, who can't live with their mums and dads.'*"

June thinks she got the idea about fostering because of her mum. "*When we lived in South Africa, people would often lose their homes if they lost their jobs and my mother would take them in for a few weeks while they got back on their feet. I wanted to help people too.*" She says, "*I knew I didn't want to be a nurse, like my mum was, but I wanted to care for children who needed it. I wanted to be needed, I think.*"

After she had had her own children, she and her husband felt it was the right time to go for it. "*I said to my husband, I'm going to grab the bull by the horns - I'm going to do it.*"

Some children haven't had a normal life

So far, she and Peter have had six placements. In the main these have been for very short periods, like overnight or for a few days. June feels that so far they haven't had to deal with anything too challenging.

"*All our placements have been fine really. One boy came to us for four days while his mum had an operation. He was high on sugar, was climbing the walls. He was used to having huge amounts of sugar on his cereal and in tea and on the* first night he just ran around the whole house. So I reduced the sugar in his tea and on his breakfast. He was quite happy and on the second day he was calmer and by the third day he was a really pleasant little boy. When I returned him to his mum, she was like, 'what have you done to him?' She seemed quite impressed."

The little girl currently living with June and Peter has been a bit more of a handful. "She was a screamer. She'd scream if she didn't get what she wanted and she'd bite and kick you too. It was what she was used to doing at home. It took us about a month to get her behaviour under control. We'd just tell her, 'if you want something, you ask nicely for it, say please and thank you.' She didn't know what please and thank you was. She would growl at you or go for you with her nails. Eventually, though, she realised her behaviour wasn't getting her anywhere. Then one day she said 'could I have a bag of crisps please?' and I nearly fell over! That was a major breakthrough."

June thinks that people need to understand where the child is coming from. "People think that saying please and thank you is just normal life but some children haven't had a normal life. They don't know it's not acceptable to lie on the floor and scream if they don't get their own way."

You've either got it or you haven't

June says, "to be a foster carer, you either take things like that on the chin and get on with it or you can take it to heart and start worrying the child doesn't like you, doesn't want to be living with you. You've got to remember the child's with *you for their own safety. You've got to do the best with the situation and get on with it."*

"Some people say it takes a special kind of person to foster. I think you've either got it or you haven't. All the training in the world won't give you the qualities you need."

She believes that these qualities include, "things like resilience and empathy for the children. But not sympathy. You don't want to be thinking 'I feel so sorry for the little mite.' You can't feel like that because if you start letting your emotions get to you, you might make silly mistakes and open up too much. If a child who's been through a lot finds your weak spot they will aim at it and they will knock you down. You've got to be loving and show your feelings, yes, but you've also got to be careful not to let your wall down. It doesn't make you a hard person."

But, June says, it's important to involve your whole family. "You need to make sure your own children are all onboard. It's not just you that's fostering, it's the whole family. Even if your children live away from home. You want them to be able to visit with your grandchildren after all. And you have to be careful – these children have often been through such bad experiences, they can be unpredictable. The whole family has to understand the issues so they can make sure everyone's safe. Luckily, all my children are really happy with us fostering."

I knew it wasn't going to be all sugar-coated

June knew before she started that fostering wasn't going to be "all roses, all sugar-coated, my eyes were open *beforehand.*"

She thinks it's important people don't go into expecting "*sweet little babies.*" She says, "*the children are mostly very disrupted and need strong boundaries and lots of love and attention. It's not like taking your sister's children for the afternoon. You have to be aware that some of these children haven't had any niceness in their lives. You have to be really strong, and have your eyes open.*"

Make one little change

So what does June get out of fostering? "*You see the child who has come from quite a bad background - they have nothing, no toys, no clothes and the look on their face when they get a new top. It might be the smallest of things but they treasure it, they hold on to it - for them this is like gold. The look on their face is the best reward.*"

"*Or the first time a child smiles or even breaks down and cries. It sounds odd, I know, but when a child who has suppressed their feelings breaks down and cries that's such a reward. People say 'you're happy that the child's crying?!' And I say 'Yes because that's a breakthrough.' The day our little boy cried, I sat there and laughed. Because he'd never cried. That feeling was better than any feeling I've had in a long time. It felt like - I've done something and that child has been able to show an emotion – to me that's the best thing since sliced bread.*"

"*Even just getting a child to sit and eat a meal at the table. Someone might think that's the norm, but if they've never sat at a table before then using a knife and fork is actually quite* an achievement. It's all about making a little change. If you can make one change in that child before they move on then you've done something - something good has come out of it."

It's my calling

June says, "the child will remember that one thing that you did for them. They'll remember that you wanted them here. That you did it because you wanted to do it. That's why I don't like fostering being called a job. This isn't my job – I do it because I want to."

"I foster because I'm helping, helping families to have children reunited with them. I want to help families and I want children to go home. If they can't go home, then we help the children to move on to adoption or long term fostering."

"I do it because this is my calling."

5. Types of foster care

Children come into foster care with very different needs. They might need somewhere to stay in an emergency – perhaps if a parent has gone into hospital suddenly and there's nowhere else they can go. They might, in these circumstances, only need fostering for a few days or weeks. Other children might need support for longer periods, for instance in cases where suspected abuse is being investigated. Some children will be unable to return to their own families at all. They might need fostering for the rest of their childhood or need supporting until suitable adoptive parents are found for them.

The age of the child (ranging from 0 to 18) when they come into care, whether they have brothers and sisters and whether they have any special needs will also make a significant difference to the sort of care and the skills needed to support them.

All of this means that fostering agencies have to provide a range of different types of foster care in order to meet children's diverse and sometimes complex needs. This chapter looks at the range of options available and how the decision is made about which type of fostering is right for you.

Not all agencies offer all forms of foster care – it depends on the needs of the children in their care. Sometimes these types of foster care are given different names.

Full-time foster care

This is the most common form of foster care. It involves looking after the day-to-day needs of a child who lives in the foster carer's home full-time. Full-time care can be provided for short or long periods depending on the child's needs. The different types of full-time care that foster carers provide are:

Emergency fostering: when a child needs somewhere to stay at very short notice. Emergency foster care is usually only for a few days, while the fostering agency finds a more long-term arrangement.

Short-term fostering: when a child needs somewhere to stay for a few weeks or months up to a couple of years. This usually results from problems or illness in the family, or from the child being harmed or abused. The foster carer will look after them while the fostering agency works to return the child to their home or move the child to an alternative permanent family. The foster carer will often need to help the child keep in contact with their family.

Long-term fostering: when a child needs somewhere to stay for the rest of their childhood. In circumstances where parents are unable to protect their children from harm, those children will not be able to return to live with them even though they may want to. Long-term foster carers give children the chance to grow up in a safe and supportive environment, where they'll receive the care and attention they need through to adulthood, while supporting them to keep in touch with their family. This is sometimes called Permanent Fostering.

Multi-dimensional treatment foster care: a specialist type of foster care for children and young people who have complex behavioural needs. It is a structured programme of care to help troubled children address their behaviour and other problems. The foster carer is supported by other professionals such as psychologists and educational specialists. Not all fostering agencies provide this type of care.

Remand foster care: sometimes young people who have committed a criminal offence and are on remand need a place to stay. It is usually foster carers who have some experience in this area that will provide this type of foster care.

Parent and child fostering: this is where a foster carer provides a home for a young parent and their baby.

Part-time foster care

Otherwise known as short break or respite fostering, this is when a child stays with a foster carer on a part-time basis, perhaps one weekend a month or one night a week, primarily to give the child's family a break. In most cases, the part-time carer provides this regular support to the same child so that they develop a good relationship.

This type of care provides valuable support particularly to disabled children and their families. It enables the child's parents to spend time with their other children, or with each other. It's also a good way for children and young people to increase their independence.

Fostering different age groups

Children have very different needs depending on their age. Foster carers tend, therefore, to be approved to care for children in a particular age range to suit their skills, experience and preference.

Here are some of the options:

Fostering babies and toddlers: involves intensive one-to-one care, responding to the child's needs. Some babies may have significant medical problems as a result of neglect or the parent being addicted to drugs or alcohol. Foster carers will work with other professionals to make sure they get the medical attention they need.

A key part of your role might be to help prepare the child to be adopted. This might mean spending time with their prospective adoptive parents.

Fostering school-age children: involves providing the support and guidance the child needs to be healthy, develop skills and get the most out of their education. On a practical level, you will take children to and from school and other activities. You are also likely to be helping the child to maintain a relationship with their own family.

Fostering teenagers: involves looking after a young person at a critical stage in their lives. Without appropriate guidance and support, there is a risk they might get into behaviour and lifestyles that could seriously affect their future.

Teenagers need foster carers who are tolerant, patient and flexible, but who can also set clear and consistent boundaries. As well as providing emotional support you will help them prepare for adulthood by developing the practical skills they'll need in the future, like cooking and managing money. Helping them stay in contact with their family is also crucial for teenagers.

Fostering children with special needs

Some children who need foster care have medical conditions or physical or learning disabilities, such as hyperactivity, autism, attention deficits, or reading difficulties. They may need special medication or care routines, or extra support with mobility or learning, for instance.

Foster carers who look after children with special needs

don't have to have any particular qualifications or previous experience. Fostering agencies will provide the support and training a foster carer might need to be able to look after a disabled child.

Parent and baby fostering

Sometimes it is both a young parent and their child who need the support of a foster carer.

You'll provide help and encouragement to both without taking over the parent's responsibility to their baby. You'll help them to develop the maturity and skills they need to live independently with their child.

Fostering unaccompanied minors

Sometimes accommodation is needed for children who are on their own and new to this country. They may be seeking asylum. Foster carers provide them with a comfortable, stable and healthy place to stay while their asylum application or other issues are dealt with. Fostering agencies will try to place these children with foster carers who share their language and culture, if possible.

Fostering brothers and sisters

Keeping brothers and sisters together can be crucial to their wellbeing. They often rely on each other for comfort and security and separation can be highly traumatic. Obviously foster carers looking after two or three children or a large sibling group will need to have the space in their homes to do so.

Fostering more than one child at a time

Many foster carers look after more than one child at a time. These children are not always related. Obviously, you'll need to have the room in your home and in your life to foster more than one child.

Deciding which type of foster care you do

Before you are approved as a foster carer, during the assessment and preparation process, the fostering agency will work closely with you to decide what type of fostering and what age and number of children are right for you and your family. This will depend on your skills and experience, the space you have available at home and whether you have other commitments, such as your own children and job.

So it will be up to you, in consultation with the agency, to decide what sort of fostering you can provide. However, it's worth bearing in mind that agencies will be conscious of needing to provide homes for specific children with specific needs and therefore are likely to prioritise those applicants who are more likely to be able to offer the sort of care they're looking for. For instance, many agencies need more foster carers for teenagers and sibling groups. Understanding the agency's priorities and being open and flexible about what you might be able to offer will help both parties make the right decision.

Remember:

- Children need foster care for many different reasons and need to be looked after for different lengths of time.

- There are different types of foster care that you could provide including short-term, long-term and short break fostering.

- Children of different ages have different needs, as do siblings and children with special needs.

- Foster carers are approved for a particular type of foster care and for a particular age range and number of children.

- The type of foster care that someone provides is based on their skills, experience, other commitments, space in their house and their preference.

- The decision about what type of fostering you do is made jointly between you and your chosen fostering agency. It is made during the assessment process.

- Some agencies need to prioritise certain types of foster care, in order to meet the needs of the particular children in their care. You may need, therefore, to be flexible about the type of care you'll consider doing.

6. David's story

"I look after teenagers. It's the age group where I feel I can make the most significant difference."

David is 52 and a single carer. He's been fostering for over 15 years, initially alongside his wife but after they divorced, he continued to foster on his own. He lives in the north east of England and fosters for his local council. He provides emergency foster care to teenage boys.

He says, *"I'm not certain why I became a foster carer. I think it had a bit to do with my background. I didn't have a bad upbringing but while I had a wonderful mother, my father was a difficult person. I think part of the reason why I decided to foster was that I thought it would be good to help others who were having a difficult childhood."*

"*It wasn't until I started fostering that I realised that what I thought was a bad father was actually quite mild! If adults went through what some of these children have been through – I don't think they could handle it at all.*"

"*When you start fostering, it certainly is an eye-opener. I know that what I accept now as the norm is completely different to what I might have accepted before becoming a foster carer. A child may be involved in drugs or drink or this, that and the other. It doesn't come as a shock to me now but before it would have done.*"

You need to treat each child as an individual

David believes it's important to treat the children with respect.

He says, "*When a child arrives with you, you have all this information on them. And sometimes it's really bad. I remember one lad, a few years back, whose report was horrendous. He came to me on remand for some pretty serious crimes. I remember saying to my wife 'we've got Hannibal Lector arriving.' That's how bad it looked. And yet, the truth of it was when he arrived, he couldn't have been nicer.*"

"*The important thing is to treat each child as an individual. Start with a clean slate and treat them with respect. That way you get back what you put in. So, yes, you've got to read up on their background and be aware of the possibilities but you've also got to go into the placement with an open mind. It's really important to treat the child based on what he could be rather than what he has been. On that basis, there isn't a* child I'd refuse to have."

David provides emergency foster care – looking after children for short periods of time. "*The majority of the children often stay for no more than a few weeks. As such you've got to be prepared for whoever and whatever walks through that door. You need to have the right attitude towards the youngster and understand that the position they're in is nine times out of ten down to their past experiences, how badly people have treated them.*"

"*That's not to say that you shouldn't take precautions. I have a safe, for instance and a keypad lock on my bedroom door. These children may not have been brought up to respect other people's property, so you have to be careful.*"

Teenagers are still very young and very needy

David has chosen to foster teenagers. Why? "*I foster teenagers,*" he says, "*because it's the age group where I feel I can make the most significant difference.*"

"*There is a shortage of foster carers for teenagers. People worry about what sort of behaviour they'll be faced with. You do have incidents – they might be involved in drugs, or alcohol and things of that nature. It isn't easy when they don't come back at ten, eleven o'clock and you have to call the police. They might have been living on the streets. It happens to a lot of youngsters if they haven't got a caring family around them. They tend to turn to their friends and spend a lot of time on the street. They aren't going to change overnight – they're not suddenly going to stay in when their pals are out. But with the right encouragement and the right atmosphere you can break these habits."*

"Like anything else, it's a question of taking time to gain their trust. Through perseverance and showing that you care, you can make small inroads. Most kids on the street don't want to be on the streets but they don't have any alternative. Your job is to give them an alternative."

"When it comes down to it, teenagers are still very young, they're still very needy. They might put on a hard face, a hard attitude but deep down like everyone else they just want to be liked. It's just about cracking open that egg so that they feel they can be liked and allow you to like them. That's the secret of success."

There are no guarantees

On the topic of success, David continues, *"it's very difficult in fostering to measure success. You certainly don't get thanks or praise, at least not from the children."*

So, how do you know whether you've made any sort of difference to a child, when they've only been with you for such a short time?

David says, *"part of the thing with fostering is you can never know. There are no guarantees. You can only hope that you made a difference to them, that you've made a breakthrough."*

"Sometimes, sadly, these lads end up in prison and you feel as if you've failed them in some way. But I got a letter from one lad recently – he must have been with me more than 8

years ago and he wasn't with me for very long. But he wrote and said 'I remember you.' He still recalled me after all these years. I think that's what matters. I was part of his timeline and I made a difference in his life. That's what's important. You can't put their lives right, you can't create miracles. But you can at least give them a happy period in their life that they can look back on."

"I looked after these two brothers who were 14 and 13, who stayed with me for a couple of years. They were quite a handful! I had to report them as missing a few times. But years down the line, one of them, who's now married with kids and a self-employed builder, came back and built my extension!"

"That's what keeps me going. Just the fact that they call years afterwards is enough to know you've made a difference in their lives and that's all you can expect really. You've played a part in their lives and they remember. And they've taken the trouble to come back and tell you that."

I get them to laugh at me

How does David help a child feel at home?

"For me," he says, "it comes down to laughter. When the child first arrives, they're very nervous. So I've got to break the ice quickly and I'll do that through laughter. I get them to laugh at me! And I'll explain to them – 'my job is purely to help you.' I say this right at the beginning and then throughout the placement. 'Remember I'm here purely to help you – I'll do whatever I can for you.'"

"At a review recently, the reviewing officer asked me what

was the most important thing about fostering. I said when I hear a child laughing and I know he's happy. Then I know he's at home here."

David thinks that, *"your approach with any child should be friendly, joyful and warm. Because if you can make them happy in the placement, you're 90% there. If someone's happy you can work with them. And if they're happy you can be happy."*

Whether you're single or in a couple you can do it equally as well

David's in a fairly unusual position of having experienced fostering as both a single carer and in a partnership. What are the pros and cons of each?

"As a single carer," he says, *"you can spend more time one-to-one with the child. Sometimes there are lads who simply get on better with a man so you can be more successful with them on your own. Sometimes it's better to have a woman present. It depends on the individual child. If you're a couple you need to have a strong working partnership and not let the child get in between you but if you've got that it can work very well."*

David thinks that, *"really it comes down to attitude rather than whether you're in a couple or not. If you've got the right attitude it doesn't matter whether you're male or female, single or in a couple, you can do it equally as well."*

You have to keep calm

"It's how the child perceives you that's important," David

says. "*For example – if you took a child to a restaurant and they started a daft carry-on like youngsters do, throwing food around etc. how would you react? You'd probably kick off a bit because you're embarrassed at the scene they're making.*"

"*But you've got to stop and consider whether you're reacting more because of how you feel, because you're embarrassed, rather than because that's the best way to deal with the situation.*"

"*You've got to recognise how you respond to things like that and try not to react on the spur of the moment. You need to keep calm and consider your next move.*"

"*But then, I've always been very laid-back. That helps, I think. You've got to be able to take everything in your stride.*"

You have to be prepared to wait

David's advice to people thinking about becoming foster carers is that "*it's very enjoyable. It can be difficult, but is also rewarding in an exceptional way.*"

"*There's a joy in knowing you've made a difference in someone's life. It sounds insignificant but it's not. It gives you a great deal of satisfaction. But you have to be prepared to wait – it might take years to find out how your care helped someone, sometimes you never know.*"

7. Choosing who to work for

As we saw in chapter one, foster carers can either work for their local council or for an independent fostering provider (IFP). It is up to you to choose which you'd prefer and it's a good idea to do your research before approaching the organisation you're interested in. This chapter considers the differences between working for a council and an independent provider and will give you some tips on how to assess which is right for you.

Working for your local council

Just to recap, your local council (or HSC trust in Northern Ireland) is responsible for all 'children in care' in your area. This means it is also responsible for finding suitable foster carers to meet the needs of those children. To do so it will want to recruit foster carers from the local area. If it does not have enough foster carers or suitable carers for the children who need them it will look to place those children with independent fostering providers.

Some people prefer to work for their local council because they feel they're part of the team responsible for the overall welfare of all children in care locally. They like the fact that a child placed with them will be from the local area because this means that the child isn't too far from their family, school and friends and social worker. In the main, councils tend to prefer to place children with the carers they have recruited directly, only buying the service from an IFP if they are unable to find the right placement from amongst their own recruits. This means local council foster carers are less likely to experience lengthy breaks between placements. This is important because foster carers are only paid when they have a child living with them.

Working for an independent fostering provider

An independent fostering provider is a private or voluntary organisation that recruits, trains and supports its own team of foster carers. These carers will look after children that the local council has been unable to place in-house.

Some people prefer to work with an independent fostering provider. They like the dedicated focus on fostering and the additional support this provides. They also like the fact that, in most cases, the child placed with them is a considered match for their level of experience and skills. Some people like working for agencies that specialise in their area of fostering interest such as caring for children with disabilities.

Doing your research

Your first port of call when researching your fostering options is probably the internet. Searching using terms like 'fostering' and 'foster care' are likely to generate a huge number of results, including lots of different fostering agencies. Your local council should be relatively easy to find in the listings but the sheer number of independent fostering providers can be confusing. How do you choose which one to approach?

Firstly, in the same way as you wouldn't call the first plumber you found in the telephone directory, you should be wary of taking your search results at face value. Coming top of the search does not mean an organisation is somehow better than another. In fact some organisations pay to appear in the top few slots. You'll need to look behind the headlines to really find out more about each agency.

Here are some of the things it will be useful for you to investigate:

Location: one of the key things to check is that a particular agency is based or has offices in your local area. If they only have branches in London and you're in North Yorkshire, for example, they may not be the right choice for you. The British Association of Adoption and Fostering (BAAF) lists those fostering providers that are BAAF members on its website (baaf.org.uk/agencies) which you can search by location. The Fostering Network's Find a Fostering Service is another really useful resource (www.fostering.net/providers).

Specialism: some IFPs specialise in terms of the sort of foster care they offer, e.g. for children under seven, sibling groups, or children with disabilities. So make sure the agency offers the sort of foster care you're interested in doing. Local councils are likely to provide the widest range of foster care.

Performance: make sure you check out the inspection reports for those agencies you're interested in (see Helpful Resources). These will give you information on how well that agency is performing against Government regulations and standards. This applies to both councils and IFPs.

Service level: ask IFPs if they are on your local council's preferred supplier list or 'framework agreement.' This is effectively a list that councils have of providers they are happy to use. If an independent fostering provider is on this list, it means the council is confident in the service level it provides. If it is not on the list, the provider may struggle to guarantee that you will not have gaps inbetween placements.

Getting more information

Much of this information will be on the organisation's website but don't shy away from contacting them directly if you have any questions. Many will also have brochures or leaflets they can send you with more details.

Find out if the agencies you're interested in are running any information events that you could attend. These can be a great way to meet staff and current foster carers and get a real feel for that organisation.

If you already know someone who fosters then ask them who they work for and whether they'd recommend the agency. They'll be well-placed to give you the low-down on an organisation.

Remember:

- As a foster carer, you can work either for your local council or an independent fostering provider. It is up to you which you choose.

- Local councils are responsible for all the children in care in their area. They are likely to place children with their own team of foster carers first, if they can.

- If local councils can't find a suitable foster home with their own team of carers, they will look to those independent fostering providers they have 'on their books' to provide carers instead.

- Independent fostering providers are private or voluntary organisations that have recruited their own team of foster carers.

- It's a good idea to do some research before deciding which agency to apply to so that you are sure they're right for you.

- Check the inspection report for any agency you're considering to make sure they are providing a good quality of service.

- If you're thinking about working for an independent fostering provider, make sure they're on your local council's 'framework agreement' as this will determine both their level of service and whether they will be able to provide continuous placements.

8. Adele's story

"You have to be ready for anything. Every placement brings its own challenges. I like not knowing what's coming through the front door!"

Adele is a single mum of three daughters, who have all grown up and left home. She fosters for an independent fostering provider and lives in the north west of England.

She has always wanted to foster. She first became aware of fostering when she was at school. One of her friends' parents fostered and Adele got to know one of their foster children quite well.

As an adult, she worked with vulnerable children with special educational needs in schools and as part of an autism outreach team. But she found it frustrating when the good work she did with vulnerable children was often undone when they went home. "*It was always in the back of my mind - what difference could I make if I could take these children home with me?*"

She was approved as a foster carer in 2010 and has looked after around 17 children since then. She's approved to take up to three children of any age and provides many types of foster care including respite, short-term, long-term and mother and baby.

Choosing who to work for

Adele feels that one of the main decisions for someone considering becoming a foster carer is whether to foster for the local council or an independent provider. She feels that often, unfortunately, the decision comes down to finances. "*I gave up a well-paid job to foster and that was a major gamble. With an independent agency you can be without placements for some time and if it's your only source of income it can be really stressful, even untenable. Whereas if you're with the council you're never going to be without a placement. But for me it was about support as well. I do know of carers who have given up because they haven't got the support they needed.*"

She says she did a lot of research into different agencies. She chose the one she works for "*because it was small, and had a very good Ofsted report. They came across as very friendly and supportive.*"

"*They've always been at the end of the phone, they're aware of my children and their needs — everyone is so I don't need to explain every time. I had a problem a while back and*" *wanted to talk to someone there and she came out the next morning to see me. I'd only expected a phone call."*

Adele believes that a key area where foster carers need support is how best to help children whose past experiences have made it difficult for them to form attachments with the people caring for them. *"The agency I work for has a real insight into this - how children with attachment problems behave and how best to help them. So I've felt very supported. There's lots of training on attachment. So you start to be able to recognise the signs."*

She says, *"whether you work for a local council or an independent agency, you have to have faith that they will place children with you that you can cope with. So, in some ways, it's their responsibility to make sure the child fits with your family. You've also got to have faith that the support you need will be there."*

It's quite an eye opener

Adele acknowledges that despite her previous experience working with vulnerable children she didn't appreciate how challenging fostering would be. *"When I worked in primary school one of my roles was to oversee those pupils who were in care. So I felt I had a good idea about how they're affected by their experiences. But I wasn't really prepared and it's quite an eye opener. Sometimes when I speak to people considering becoming foster carers they seem to think 'well I've got a spare room, and two children already so another one isn't going to make a great deal of difference.' They think it will be just an extension of their own* family without taking into consideration the background of these children, what they've been through and how that's going to impact on them."

Every placement brings its own challenges

Adele's had a wide range of children placed with her. She had a period with lots of very short-term stays as well as providing respite care. She's cared for children from a range of ages and with very different needs.

She says, "you have to be ready for anything. I enjoy the challenge and every placement brings its own challenges. I like not knowing what's coming through the front door!"

She now has three children placed with her, all of whom will stay long-term. They're aged five, nine and eleven.

"They are gelling together nicely as a family group," she says. "The challenge is getting it right for these children because you are their family now. You've got to help them get over all the issues that they have faced. My job is to make this permanent family arrangement work and help them to become well-rounded individuals."

She says each child has their own way of dealing with what's happened to them. For instance the oldest prefers to be on his own. "He would rather spend time in his bedroom, out of the way. It's because he doesn't know how to form relationships really. So he stays away from them. My challenge is to bring him into the family, help him understand that it's ok to trust other people, to rely on other people."

"I do this by giving him time alone with me. But I do this in *ways that won't feel too threatening to him. I know what his interests are – he loves animals for instance so I'll find a wildlife programme on telly that might interest him and say 'why don't you come and watch this with me?' It's about finding opportunities to help him to realise it's ok to sit and talk to somebody, to rely on somebody. Also, I'm always asking about how his day's been. Not 'how was your day?' but 'how did you get on in that maths test you had this morning?' – so that he knows that I've been thinking about him during the day, I care enough about him to wonder what's been going on with him while we've been apart."*

Adele's youngest foster child has very different challenges. She says, *"if you read his profile, most people wouldn't want to take him on. But he is a fantastic little character, an amazing little boy with a massive personality. But he has major challenges – he's very hyperactive and if he doesn't want to do something, it's difficult to get him to do it. He can be aggressive. Plus, as a result of his early childhood experiences he is indifferent to pain. He doesn't recognise pain as pain so he has no caution, no fear, he can harm himself without realising it."*

So what does she do to help him? *"It's difficult to explain to a five year old who doesn't understand what pain is, but whenever the opportunity arises I'll use it. For instance, if he does hurt himself then I'll try to describe to him how that might feel – 'that must feel quite stingy or hot or throbby' - to make him more aware of what's happened. At school if other children hurt themselves the teachers will say to him – 'oh look so-and-so's bumped their head, look they're rubbing their head, it must really hurt and that's why they're crying.'"*

She believes that children benefit from foster care because it gives them a sense of security that "*they've got someone they know they can be themselves with, that it doesn't matter what they do or what they say I will still care about them. They haven't always had that. For children to become secure with who they are they need someone who cares about them regardless.*"

The pros and cons of being a single carer

Adele believes there are benefits to being a single foster carer, but of course there are negatives too. "*Obviously the cons are that you are on your own,*" she says. "*There are some things you can't talk to your friends about because you'd be breaking confidentiality. Whereas a couple would be able to discuss things openly together.*" Also there are practical issues: "*if you want to pop out to the shops you have to take the children with you.*"

But there are pros to it as well. "*Children can be manipulative, they'll play one parent off against the other. Well, they can't do that with me! Plus, one thing the children really need is consistency and if, as a couple, you're not parenting in a consistent way, I could imagine that could lead to some real difficulties. There are also some children who are better off in a single-parent household, because of their past experiences.*"

You need to put aside what's happened in the past

Adele acknowledges that it can sometimes be difficult working with the child's parents but, she says, "*you need* to put aside what's happened in the past, be non-judgmental. Whatever's happened, they are that child's family and you have to respect that. It puts the child in a really difficult position if they think you're against their parents, makes them feel caught in the middle, as if they're being disloyal to their parents. You've got to work with them in the best way you can."

The little daily rewards that make all the difference

Adele says that the rewards that come with fostering are the small daily signs of change and improvement, "the little things that people with their own children would take for granted."

She gives a recent example: "This morning the youngest, very hyperactive child with no concentration at all - I left him alone for two minutes and when I came back he was sat at the table colouring. He had chosen to do that and that for him is a major achievement. He had chosen to sit down and do that rather than bounce around the furniture."

And another: "The first time the oldest boy threw a bit of a strop and slammed his door was, for me, a real 'yes!' moment. It meant that he was now settled and confident enough that he knew I would still care about him even if he went off and slammed the door. It was a major step forward."

Love is not enough

What does it take to be a foster carer? "People think all

you have to do is give these children love and they'll be fine but love is not enough. You need more skills than that but you do get love back. And when he puts his arms around me and says 'I love you mummy,' there's nothing better than that."

Adele feels the key skill you need is patience. *"There can be times when someone is having a meltdown, screaming at you, telling you they hate you and you have to take it all and you can't take it personally, you have to separate what's going on at that moment and understand why it's going on and that it's all part of a process, it's all part of what has gone on before for them and how that's impacting on who they are now. And you have to remain calm."*

"If people have the skills and the patience and it was something they knew enough about to make that educated decision and they felt it was something they really could do then I'd say do it. It's been the best thing I've ever done. It's been a very challenging four years for me but then I like a challenge and I'd never go back."

9. Becoming a foster carer

Foster care is such a crucial role it's vital that fostering agencies do everything they can to ensure that foster carers have the time, space and ability to do it well. That's why there is a rigorous assessment process that all prospective foster carers must complete.

Unlike most other jobs you might apply for, where it is your skills and experience that an employer is most interested in, there are many more factors to take into account with the role of foster carer. Given you'll be taking a child or children into your home and looking after them 24/7, the assessment process also needs to be able to evaluate whether your home is suitable and that you have the time to care for them properly.

By building up a detailed picture of you, your family, your home and your lifestyle, the fostering agency will be able to evaluate whether a child would be safe and well looked after in your care as well as making sure you have the skills and the temperament to cope with the challenges this role can bring.

Assessments should be completed within eight months (ref: Department of Education). To the prospective foster carer this can feel like a frustratingly long time, but it's worth remembering that this also gives you, the applicant, the time to get a detailed understanding of what being a foster carer entails and to develop some of the skills you'll need.

This chapter will go through the key stages of the assessment process so that you know what to expect, what you'll have to do and why.

Registering your interest

Once you've chosen an agency, the first step is to register your interest in fostering with them. You're not committing to anything at this stage but it's when the process really starts.

Some agencies will ask you a few basic questions at this stage – for instance whether you have a spare room to accommodate a child. This helps them to make sure that you meet the basic criteria before proceeding any further.

If the agency is prioritising applications from people wishing to do particular types of foster care then it should advise you of this at the outset. If their priority and yours don't match, then they may well be able to point you in the direction of another agency which might be more appropriate.

Pre-screening

This involves a preliminary evaluation of whether or not you're a suitable candidate to go forward to the detailed formal assessment stage. Its purpose is to make sure that there is a good chance of you being approved before committing the time and resources required to assessing your candidacy in greater detail. At this stage the agency will want to check that there aren't any basic or significant reasons why you couldn't foster.

The home visit

This pre-screening usually takes the form of a detailed conversation with a representative of the agency - often but not always a social worker - in your home. Often known as an initial visit, its purpose is to enable the agency to find out more about you, your family and your home. It's also your opportunity to ask lots of questions and explore any of your initial thoughts and concerns about fostering. As with all the stages of the process, it's important that you're open and honest with the agency staff.

Your discussion is likely to include the following areas:

- Why you want to foster

- What childcare or other care experience you have and your levels of understanding about children and how they develop

- Whether your house is suitable

- Your work and other commitments

- Who else lives with you

- Whether you or anyone in your household have any criminal convictions

- The role of the foster carer

- What happens next in the assessment process

- What support the agency will provide.

Stage one – completing the application form and checks

Stage one is the start of the formal assessment process. It involves you completing a detailed application form. It is also during this stage that police checks will be conducted to confirm that no one in your household has any criminal convictions that would prevent you from caring for a child.

The application form

The application form is like a job application form but much more detailed. You'll need to provide lots of information about you, your partner and your children if you have them. This will include education history, work history, current commitments and so on. You'll need to give the contact details of several referees too.

Statutory checks

When the agency has received your completed application form it will carry out a range of statutory checks including police and Disclosure and Barring Service (formerly known as Criminal Records Bureau/CRB) checks (this is in England. For Scotland it's the DisclosureScotland service and in Northern Ireland it's AccessNI). These will be carried out to make sure that you, or anyone living with you, have not committed any offences that automatically disqualify you from fostering. You're likely to be asked for proof of your identity (like a passport, birth or marriage certificate) and you'll also need to have a health check to show you don't have any major health problems that would prevent you from being able to care for a child. The agency will also take up your personal and employment references.

Once all this material has been gathered and assessed, the agency will make a decision about whether to proceed with your application. It must inform you of its decision within 10 working days of having received all the information it needs to make that decision.

Stage two – training and assessment

Once the agency has confirmed that you are a suitable candidate, stage two of the assessment begins. This involves training sessions to increase your knowledge about fostering and detailed conversations with an 'assessor' over a number of weeks to build up a complete picture of you and your family and home. The final part of this process is when all the evidence gathered by the assessor is presented to a panel of independent experts to make a recommendation about whether you should be approved as a foster carer.

Pre-approval training

During this stage, you will attend pre-approval training, typically the Fostering Network's 'The Skills to Foster™' training course. It's an extremely valuable opportunity to learn about all aspects of fostering, to build up your skills and to identify areas where you might need more training and support in the future.

The training covers how abuse and neglect and being separated from their own family can affect a child's development and behaviour. It also covers how to deal with difficult behaviour and how to provide a safe environment for a vulnerable child or children.

The training is likely to involve experienced foster carers and you'll be able to meet other prospective foster carers too.

A children's session should also be provided so that the children of potential foster carers can start to understand what's involved when a foster child comes to live in their home.

The assessment

The detailed assessment stage of the process will follow completion of the training. Over the course of several weeks you will meet regularly with an assessor to discuss in detail your application to become a foster carer.

Identifying strengths and weaknesses

The assessor's job is to identify your strengths – your experience, skills and qualities. They will want you to demonstrate these strengths through practical examples. This might include talking about relevant situations you've been in or challenges you've faced, how you handled them and what you learnt from the experience.

Their job is also, of course, to identify any gaps in your experience or knowledge. It might be, for instance, that you don't have direct practical experience of a child with attachment difficulties. In these circumstances the assessor will want you to demonstrate your understanding of that issue through your discussions. They might recommend some further reading in order to boost your knowledge, might put you in touch with an experienced foster carer or suggest a practical way of building your skills like volunteering at a school or children's centre.

It's important to realise that any gaps in your experience will not necessarily prevent you from becoming a foster carer. It's all a matter of degree. If there's a major gap in your experience or abilities that might well work against you. If it's something that can be overcome with additional training or support or research though, then your assessor may make that a recommendation.

These explorations can feel a bit nerve-wracking but it's

essential to view them as positively as possible. Not only are they necessary to ensure that a child would be safe in your care but also to make sure you have a full understanding of what's involved and how you as a family will be able to cope. Many carers feel they discover an awful lot about themselves during this process which is really useful when they start looking after a child.

Talking to people who really know you

Your assessor will talk to anyone else who lives in your household including your children. They will also contact any adult children living elsewhere and any ex-partners (from long-term relationships), and gather information about you, usually via a written questionnaire and/or telephone interview. These conversations are treated as confidential and enable the assessor to check that the information you have given about your past and your parenting style is correct.

Some people worry that this means an ex-partner might scupper their application to foster by being negative about them. However, comments from all your contributors will be weighed up in relation to each other so that a fair and balanced picture is arrived at. And while this all might feel really intrusive, most people understand the need to check that an applicant is telling the truth about themselves in order to ensure the safety of vulnerable children.

Assessing the type of foster care that's right for you

During the assessment you and the assessor will discuss in depth your capacity to provide foster care given your other commitments and responsibilities.

It will also be at this stage that more detailed investigation will take place about the type of foster care you might be best suited for and the age and number of children you could and want to look after.

The report

All the information from your discussions and any written evidence are gathered by your assessor into a report which will detail your skills, your future training needs and areas where perhaps you need more help. You'll be able to see this report and add your own comments to it.

Approval

The final stage of this assessment process is the decision about whether you should be approved as a foster carer. This takes all the evidence that has been gathered into account and there are a number of people involved in this decision-making process.

The fostering panel: made up of independent representatives from the fostering agency, education and health, voluntary organisations, foster carers and independent members of the local community, the panel's role is to review the assessor's report in a meeting with you and your assessor. The panel will subsequently make a recommendation to the fostering agency as to your suitability to foster.

The fostering agency decision-maker: usually a senior member of the fostering agency team, their role is to make the final decision about whether to approve you as a foster carer based on the assessment and the panel's recommendation. If you are not approved, the decision-maker will write to you explaining the reasons for their decision, within five working days of the panel meeting.

Independent review mechanism (IRM): the IRM is an independent body which evaluates applications by people who have been turned down by a fostering agency following stage two of the assessment process. If you want to appeal against the decision made about you, you can contact either the agency decision-maker or the IRM (but not both). The IRM will review all the evidence and meet with you to discuss your application before making a recommendation about whether the decision should be overturned. The final decision will be made by the fostering agency.

Remember:

- There is a standard assessment process that all fostering agencies must follow to check the suitability of candidates to become foster carers. It has been developed to make sure that vulnerable children will be safe and well cared for.

- The first step is to register your interest with your chosen agency. An agency representative will visit you in your home to do an initial check that you are suitable to proceed to the next stage.

- You'll be asked to complete a detailed application form and then the agency will carry out statutory checks and verify your references.

- The next stage is the formal assessment when an assessor will visit you over a number of weeks to gather evidence about your suitability to foster.

- During the assessment process you will receive training on key aspects of fostering and meet other potential carers.

- Details of your family life, your work commitments, childcare commitments, home environment will be discussed and evaluated alongside an assessment of your skills and qualities to see whether you would be suitable to be a foster carer.

- The assessment process takes time, patience and commitment but also provides a valuable opportunity for you to develop your understanding and your skills.

10. Natalie's story

"The perception is that you have to jump through lots of hoops to become a foster carer but I didn't find that. It was such a valuable process."

Natalie is 34 and married with two children under five. She and her husband have been fostering since early 2013. So far, they have fostered one four-month-old boy who stayed with them for seven months. She lives in the south east of England.

One day, she and her husband realised they'd both been thinking about fostering for quite some time. *"It felt like the right time to do it. I was stepping back from my career to spend time with my own children but also, it just felt like — the time is now. We could wait but who knows where we might be in five or ten years time? We felt that if we have the* capacity and something to offer now, then we should do it now."

Natalie and her husband chose to work for their local council. "*I really want to do it for the children and not for the money. We're fortunate to be in a good financial position so we can do that. It's a moral thing for us, we want to support state care – we feel that's how it should be done.*"

The team got to know us in such a lot of detail

Natalie says they were really impressed with the process they went through to be approved as carers. "*The perception is that you have to jump through lots of hoops to become a foster carer but I didn't find that. It was such a valuable process and quite validating for us. The team got to know us in such a lot of detail, which I suppose some might find intrusive, but it's because they want to understand what makes you tick and what your strengths and weaknesses are. They want to know that you understand the challenges, that you understand how your own childhood experiences affect your resilience and how you parent. I actually found it really enjoyable.*"

Natalie feels the process helped them to know themselves and prepared them mentally for what it was going to be like to foster. "*It was very practical, very one-to-one.*"

"*I feel I know myself better – I know from the process that I'm a resilient person. And that self-knowledge is a useful resource to call upon when it gets difficult. For instance, I* have felt at times 'this is so hard, this is more than anybody can be asked to do' but then I'd think - if I can't handle it and I'm one of the most resilient people I know – well I'd better stick with it."

It's still a real learning curve

Even though the assessment process and the training helped them to feel really prepared, Natalie says that they're definitely still learning.

"When we did the training we learnt a lot about attachment. But despite that, we still underestimated the impact it can have. Our first placement was a four month old boy and I thought because he was so young that he wouldn't be affected. It was only as time went on that we realised that the constant crying and his need to be held all the time was due to his past experiences."

"We were naïve really. We had him for seven months and it's only now when I look back can I see it more clearly. It was such a bombshell when he first arrived with us. He didn't make eye contact, would push his head away."

"Over time we got more information about his background and we were able to piece things together with his behaviour. And over those seven months, he improved such a lot."

"The big thing I wasn't expecting was that because I really love babies, I thought I would be in love with the child straight away and I wasn't at all. I was acutely aware all the time of the difference between him and my own children and spent a lot of time wrestling with guilt. In the end I had to look that feeling in the eye and realised that it was natural to feel like *this, it takes a bit more work, a bit more time for that feeling to come."*

Saying goodbye

"By the time it came to him moving on," Natalie says. *"I felt very different. I felt incredibly responsible for him. As he left he was waving at us — he'd only just learnt to wave and we felt so proud of him, of how far he'd come. It was so lovely to see him wave and smile."*

"But of course, what's strange is that having developed these feelings for him over the time he'd been with us, you then have to switch them off when he moves on."

"You just have to remember that you've helped them a couple of steps along a really long journey. And you have to trust that it's the right move for them."

You need to be resilient

Natalie thinks that people shouldn't *"underestimate how difficult it is caring for a child who is not your own. You haven't got those reserves of love to draw on."* She says, *"you need to be really resilient — you do get frustrated and upset but you have to remember why you're doing it and not get too worked up."*

She believes that the training was really helpful with this. *"It keeps you in the zone,"* she says. *"It keeps you focused on the perspective of the child all the time, which is important."*

Natalie says, *"the child is so disconnected. That's the tragedy really of them being in care, you just have the child, and it's your job to help them get to the next step, make the most of them in the short time you have them."*

She adds that, *"you do need the support of your family, their encouragement – 'you're doing so well, keep going.' Some of the members of our family were rather sceptical which meant we didn't feel like we could really let on how difficult it actually was, which was hard."*

It's lovely to see him with people to whom he's really special

She comments that there was a lot of interaction with the child's family. *"This is often the case with babies,"* she says. *"The meetings can be tense and sometimes I'd feel a bit low after them but in other ways it was lovely to see him with people to whom he's really special. You see them taking pictures of him and so on."*

The hardest thing we had to do

She closes by saying, *"probably the hardest thing we had to do was to make the decision to foster in the first place. It felt like we were taking a leap of faith. But once we'd made the decision, it felt much better. We realised we could do it."*

11. Looking after a foster child

So you've been approved as a foster carer. Congratulations! But here, of course, is where the hard work really starts.

If you've no previous experience of fostering, then this might be the aspect you're most anxious about. Perhaps you're asking yourself what it's going to be like having a foster child live with you, what sort of behaviour you might expect or what happens if the child just doesn't like you.

These are all quite natural things to worry about but the key thing to remember as you're reading this section is that you won't have reached this stage without a lot of training and a lot of support. Pre-approval training (see chapter nine) will have helped increase your understanding of the realities of foster care and given you some tools to help. The assessment process itself will have taught you a lot about what's involved and that you have the skills to do it – you wouldn't be approved otherwise. And once you are approved, you'll carry on learning and being supported with each foster child that's placed with you. So you'll be much more clued-up and confident than you might feel right now.

This chapter explores some of the realities of looking after a foster child. Starting with how a child is placed with you in the first place, it also covers what you can expect, the key aspects of looking after a foster child and your core responsibilities as a foster carer.

How a child is placed with you

During your assessment process you will have agreed with the fostering agency what type of foster care you will do. When you are approved this agreement becomes a formal contract so that all parties are clear which ages and numbers of children you can foster and within what type of foster care.

It will not be up to you to choose which particular child comes to live with you. The fostering agency will match each child with the right carers, based on the child's needs, your skills and level of experience and the make-up of your family.

You will get the opportunity to discuss the placement with your social worker and raise any concerns if you have them.

Before the child arrives with you, the agency will provide you with as much detail as they have on that child's background, the reasons why they are in care, whether they've lived with foster carers before, what the plan is for them etc.

Sometimes, however, this is not possible. Obviously if you're an emergency foster carer there may not be time to gather this information before the child arrives with you. It might be that there simply isn't much information available. If the child is very young it might be difficult to assess exactly what's happened to them and how they have been affected.

In these circumstances, you will need to adapt quickly to how the child behaves and make sure you record as much about them as possible to help the team fill in some of the gaps.

Similarly, in an ideal world, the child should also have been helped to understand a bit more about you, your family and your home before they arrive. However, again, this is not always possible so it may be that a child arrives not knowing anything about where they're going to live. You'll need to reassure them and gently introduce them to your home and household. Some of the things they might feel anxious about include:

- Who will be looking after me?
- Where will I sleep?
- Are there are any pets?
- Where can I put my stuff?
- What time is bedtime?

- Can I watch TV/go on a computer?

- Does the family know about me, what I like and dislike?

Just remember, if you're worried about what it's going to be like when this child arrives, it's nothing compared to how they feel!

What to expect

So, what should you expect when a child comes to live with you? The most obvious answer is – expect the unexpected! After all, every child is unique and will bring with them their very individual personalities, their different experiences and backgrounds and their particular set of circumstances.

Even if your fostering agency has been able to supply you with lots of information about the child before they arrive, you still can't be certain of how they will respond to you and how they will take to living in your home.

What you can expect is that, in all likelihood, they will have experienced some form of trauma, neglect or abuse in their early childhood. This can result in high levels of anxiety about what it means to be cared for. Anxiety which is often focused on their core concerns of 'am I lovable, whom can I trust, how can I avoid getting hurt?'

This anxiety and fear can be very hard for the child to handle. They often express these emotions through a range of behaviours. One child, for instance, might be withdrawn and rejecting, while another is needy.

Another might equally be perfectly behaved and highly self-reliant, while another child is volatile and angry.

They might also have problems with eating or sleeping, be hyperactive or prone to risk-taking, bed-wetting or self-harm.

Your job, at its heart, is to try and reduce the anxiety that lies beneath a child's behaviour. In doing so you'll also help them to build self-esteem, feel able to trust others to care for them and learn how to manage their emotions in more positive ways.

The foster carer toolkit

Your fostering agency should provide you with lots of information, support and training on working with children who have experienced trauma, neglect or abuse. This will include tactics for dealing with different behaviour and approaches that will help reduce the child's anxiety about being cared for.

Here are some of the key aspects of how to look after a child who is affected in this way. Consider it a toolkit that will help you provide a high level of care:

Be available: in order to help the child learn to trust in your care, you need to be a calm, attentive and reliable presence, ready to respond quickly to the child's needs.

This will need to be done in a way that feels comfortable for the child. So a cuddle might be out of the question, but sharing an activity like reading or playing means you're there for them, listening to them and helping them do something they enjoy.

You'll also need to find ways to reassure the child about time spent apart – be clear about the duration and purpose of the separation and find ways to show the child you were thinking about them while they were away.

Be consistent: you'll need to be consistent in your approach with the child to build up their confidence that they can rely on you. Establishing a daily routine is a key part of this - knowing when mealtimes and bedtimes are can help the child feel safe. All members of the household will need to work together in a consistent way to ensure the child's sense of security is maintained.

Be alert: you need to be alert to the signals the child is sending via their behaviour. Look beyond the outward signs – stay away, I don't need you, you can't help me – to the concerns that lie beneath – can I trust you? will you leave me? I need you but I'm scared.

Watch out for the situations/events/times of day that seem to trigger certain behaviour. This will provide clues about the underlying cause and help you work out ways to tackle/avoid difficult situations.

Also, be aware of how the child's behaviour makes you feel. This can help you work through any feelings of rejection or anger, for instance, as well as helping you to understand what the child is really communicating.

Be creative: children will sometimes display quite puzzling behaviour or not respond to conventional methods of handling it. Foster carers need to think creatively to work out how best to deal with a particular issue or behaviour.

You'll also need to be able to adapt to the needs of each child that is placed in your care. What works for one won't necessarily work for another.

Focus on the positive: a child in care can often have a very negative view of themselves, believing they are undeserving of love and attention. By focusing on the positive – e.g. recognising and rewarding good behaviour, encouraging them to try new things, valuing their achievements, however small, you can help to undermine their negative perceptions and start to build their self-esteem.

Be patient: it takes time for a child to realise that they can trust and rely on you. Their negative views of themselves and the trustworthiness of other people tend to be very deeply entrenched. They will be on the look-out for evidence that their view is correct.

It will, therefore, take a huge amount of patience and resilience to provide the consistent, reassuring and positive care that will help to break down these perceptions.

Don't take it personally: alongside patience, it's important that you try not to take any behaviour directed at you personally. Instead you need to recognise that behaviour for what it is.

For instance, a child might reject any attention or care

you try to give them. This can be very upsetting and difficult to deal with.

But by seeing that behaviour not as a personal criticism but as a defence mechanism, as a way the child has developed to protect themselves from further hurt, you can focus better on what the child needs from you.

Keep calm: being faced with challenging behaviour can be upsetting, it can make you feel angry or hurt.

It's important though to try and remain calm. By doing so, you'll help to take the heat out of the situation, identify any triggers that can be dealt with either straightaway or later once the child is less upset, and continue to be the reassuring presence that shows them that while you might dislike their behaviour you still care for them.

Of course, this can be extremely difficult. After all, you're not a robot! But before reacting, take a deep breath and consider what's really going on (see 'Be alert' above).

You'll also need to find other ways to blow off steam – talk it out with your partner, with a friend or with your social worker - don't deal with it alone.

Ask for help: make sure you call on the support of your social worker. That's what they're there for. They can help you work through what's been happening and help you come up with ways to address it.

Accept your limitations: as a foster carer, you're already halfway to superhero status! But you can't do it all. You can't cure the child of their past and how it's affected them. You can't be perfectly calm and patient all the time. Accept your limitations, pick yourself up, dust yourself down and keep going. Don't be afraid to seek help if you are feeling overwhelmed and frustrated.

Be proud of yourself: through good times and bad, don't forget that your presence in the child's life is invaluable. You're giving them stability and a real chance to overcome the effects of their past so they can look forward to a better life.

Your key responsibilities

As well as providing the day-to-day care that a child needs, you also play a crucial role in other significant aspects of their life. You'll help them benefit from learning and educational opportunities, help them to maintain their relationship with their own family and work to protect them from harm. You'll also keep detailed records of events which will be used to determine how they will continue to be looked after.

Supporting children's education: foster children often don't do as well in school as their peers. This is largely due to the disruption they have experienced in their lives, perhaps living in a number of different foster homes or having to move schools.

As a foster carer, then, one of your key responsibilities is to support the child to get the most out of school. You might need to take and collect them from school and you'll need to make sure they have the space, time and quiet to do their homework. You should attend parents' evenings and other events like Sports Day. It will be important to build a good relationship with their school so that everyone concerned is in a better position to deal with any issues.

You'll also need to help the child to express any concerns about school and be prepared to act on their behalf, as their advocate, so they get the support they need.

Helping children develop key skills: children in care may have fallen behind in developing basic skills. They might need help to learn things that other children their age are already adept at – like reading. They might also behave in ways more appropriate to younger children. They may lack confidence that they can do things.

You play a crucial role in providing opportunities for them to try new things, being encouraging and supportive as well as realistic about what they can achieve. You'll need to help them learn at a pace they feel comfortable with and praise their achievements.

Protecting children from harm: as we have seen it is likely that the child in your care has experienced harm in their early childhood. This may have taken different forms, including neglect, emotional and physical abuse and sexual abuse. This makes them more vulnerable and at risk from further harm in a number of ways.

They may still be in contact with people who do not have their best interests at heart or their own behaviour might put them at risk. Their past experiences might lead them to interpret aspects of normal family life as potentially harmful to them, putting foster carers themselves at risk of being accused of inappropriate behaviour.

It is an area that needs to be handled with great sensitivity. Fostering agencies will provide training and information to help you understand the implications of what's known as 'safe caring' for the child, you and your family.

Working with children's families: a hugely important part of your role is to help the child maintain a relationship with their own family.

It is the responsibility of the social work team to determine what type and frequency of contact is in the best interests of the child. In most cases, it will be face-to-face meetings but sometimes this is not appropriate and might be replaced with letters or telephone calls. Meetings may be supervised by a social worker or other professional.

It is your responsibility to support the child both practically, in terms of helping them attend face-to-face sessions or receive calls, and emotionally, in terms of helping them to deal with their feelings about seeing or hearing from their family. It's important that you give them the space to talk about their family if they want to and that you remain non-judgmental.

Keeping a record: another of the foster carer's duties

is to keep a daily record of the events in the life of the child and the rest of the household. This record is important for a number of reasons:

- It will help you to contribute clear information about the child to their social worker and the rest of the team. This will be used to inform plans about a child's future

- It will enable a child to access information about their childhood in later life

- It can provide an accurate account of events that might become significant or contentious in the future

- It may help to safeguard you and your family from false allegations

- It may be used in a court hearing.

It's important to remember that this record is not the same as a diary. It is a formal log of events that will be seen by the fostering agency/local authority and possibly the child themselves. It will be inspected and signed by your social worker regularly. It is not, therefore, the place for your thoughts and feelings about the child or those events − unless your opinion has some particular bearing. The most important thing is that the records are factual, accurate, legible and to the point.

You should keep a separate record for each child placed with you. Records should be kept somewhere safe.

Saying goodbye

Unless you are a long-term foster carer, at some point the foster child will leave your home. They might return to their own family, move on to live with adoptive parents or another foster family.

This can be an emotional time. It is, of course, entirely natural to find it hard to say goodbye to a child in whom you've invested a lot of time and energy and have come to care for a great deal.

It's important to give yourself time to come to terms with this sense of loss. Talk through your feelings with your partner, family and social worker. Other foster carers who will have been through exactly the same thing will be of particular support. Remember that you have done everything you can for the child and helped them make this important next step in their lives. Then take a deep breath and prepare yourself for the next child to arrive.

Remember:

- By the time you become a foster carer, you will have already had lots of training on how to look after the child in your care.

- Unless you are a long-term foster carer, it is the social work team who decide which child will be placed with you, based on what you're approved for and what the child needs.

- Unless you are an emergency foster carer, before the placement begins, you should receive information about the child – and the child should be told all about you. However, this is not always possible.

- Children may display a range of behaviour, some of it challenging, but often this is a reflection of feelings of anxiety and confusion about being cared for.

- A foster carer needs to be alert to what's going on beneath the surface and provide calm and reliable care in order to help the child reduce their anxiety.

- A key element of being a foster carer will be to help the child maintain a relationship with their own family. You will be supported by the social work team to do this in a way that works best for the child.

- Keeping a daily record of significant events, issues and developments in each child's life is an important part of your role.

12. Claire's story

"I expected the children to love me back or be happy that I was doing all this. I got the shock of my life."

Claire is in her 60s and has been fostering for 15 years. She is Caribbean by heritage and fostered in the US before coming to the UK. She has three daughters, one of whom is adopted, and five grandchildren. She lives in north London and is single.

Since moving to the UK in 2003 she has fostered nine children. Originally registered as a short-term carer she now fosters one child long-term and continues to offer short-term and emergency placements too.

Fostering is something that had nagged away at her for some time before she actually went for it. "*I had this dream that if I had pots of money I would buy a big mansion* and take in all these unloved kids." Eventually it was her neighbour, a foster carer, who encouraged her to think more seriously about applying.

She's currently fostering on behalf of a London borough council. She used to foster for an independent fostering provider but when the local council decided to place all their looked after children with their own foster carers, it left her without a placement for 18 months. So she moved over to the council.

I got the shock of my life

She admits she was naïve when she first started fostering. "*I went into it,*" she says, "*thinking 'here are these children who have been in this horrible situation, unloved and unwanted. And I will do all these nice things for them, give them lots of hugs and kisses, cook for them, heal all their wounds and make their lives so much better.' And in turn, I guess I expected them to love me back or, for want of a better term, be grateful, be happy that I was doing all this. I got the shock of my life.*"

Instead of receiving gratitude, the children's response was often to reject her love. "*It was one of the most difficult things for me to come to terms with – being rejected. It came,*" she says, "*as a real eye-opener to find that there were children who had been living with abuse and neglect for so long they could not understand how things could be different. They didn't know how to accept love, someone being kind to them, could not see themselves as being worthy of that love so instead of embracing it they fought against it.*"

That was very difficult for me to deal with. Initially I felt hurt – 'I'm doing all this for you, and you don't seem to care. I bought you this lovely dress and you've ripped it to pieces.'

But with time and with training, she says, "*you learn to see it's not personal, to not take it personally and you learn to persevere.*"

And after a while that perseverance pays off. "*I had this one child,*" Claire says. "*She'd been abused since she was two, came to me when she was 11 but behaved as if she was five. She could not accept love or kindness, in fact you couldn't go within three metres of her. It was very difficult for me because I'm a really tactile person. She'd been with me for six months and we'd do lots of things together like cooking, making cakes. Then one day I was in the kitchen and she came up behind me and put her arms around me. And in that instant, in that miniscule little thing I thought 'ok, maybe she's getting it, that it's ok to love and be loved.' Of course the minute I turned around she was off again but I hope that she was able to take that moment on into her future life.*"

It's all about patience

"*No two children are alike,*" Claire says. "*What will work with one won't work for another. You have to get to know each child and find out what makes them tick. Some children will walk through the door and jump into your arms and some will never do that.*"

One child Claire looked after was very aggressive and was always getting into fights at school. "*Gradually I* chipped away, chipped away and by the time she was ready to move on to a long-term placement she had totally changed. She was able to walk away from confrontation (most of the time) and to accept responsibility for her actions. I had parents coming up to me in the playground saying 'what have you done to her? She's changed so much.'"

"How did I do it? It's all about patience, about not giving up. These children feel so worthless so it's about hanging in there with them, in those rough moments, those times when they're at their lowest. You've got to keep feeding them positive thoughts, keep telling them over and over again how worthy they are, how important they are. And keep applauding their tiniest achievements. One time this girl had got into several fights but she had also been able to sit still through a lesson so rather than focusing on the fighting I said, 'Wow! You sat still through a lesson. Fantastic!'"

I'm still learning

Claire says, "I've been doing this for 15 years and I'm still learning, learning from the children really. I had one girl quite early on, and when she arrived I told her all these things she needed to do - to use a knife and fork, do this, don't do that and one day she said, 'it's too much. I can't remember all these things. I've got teachers at school telling me all different things and now you, it's too much.' And I thought, it is too much. So I stood back and thought 'ok, of all these things, which is the most dangerous, which could hurt her or someone else? So I thought of two things and I said these are the only two things I'm going to ask you to do and I told the school the same thing. After a while that began to work, she began to find it easier to take things on board. It helped that I had a good relationship with the school and we were able to work together. You need that. You can't do it alone."

Treating the child's family with respect

Claire says when it comes to the child's family, she's always "*borne in mind that they are the parents and I treat them with respect.*" She remembers one family who were distraught at having their children taken away. "*I'd had the children for a couple of weeks at the time and I said to their parents – 'you have done a fantastic job, you've got two wonderful children, well mannered and delightful.' I just felt that with everything that was going on - the police investigation, the children being taken from them, having to explain their friends and neighbours - I just felt somebody needed to say to them that it's ok. And the smile on that mum's face, I'll never forget it.*"

13. Working as a foster carer

Increasingly foster carers are viewed as professionals, performing an important role in society. This is why the job title changed from foster parent to foster carer – to recognise that foster carers do more than just parent a foster child, that there are expectations upon them to work as part of the fostering agency team, to undertake training and to develop their skills. This chapter looks at the professional aspects of the role, the team you'll be working with and the support you'll receive.

Starting life as a foster carer

Once you've been approved as a foster carer, the fostering agency is likely to give you an induction. This is an introduction to how the agency works, what is expected of you in your role as well as the initial training you will receive to develop your skills.

Policies and procedures

As part of this induction, you should receive a copy of the agency's policies and procedures and a handbook. This will include how an agency will support and train you, how it will investigate an allegation and its health and safety policies.

It's important that you take the time to go through these carefully. They will help you get a good understanding of the agency's way of working and the codes of conduct that you will need to adhere to.

Foster carer contract

After you've been approved, you'll be asked to sign a Foster Carer Contract. This is a formal agreement between you and the fostering agency detailing what is expected of you in terms of the care of the child placed with you and how you will work with the agency. It also details what you can expect from the agency in return.

Here are just a few examples of what is expected from you in relation to the child in your care:

- that you will treat them as a valued member of your family

- that you will keep them safe

- that you will encourage them to attend school and maintain contact with their family (if appropriate)

- that you will make sure the child gets any medical help they need.

In terms of working with your agency, you will be expected to, for example:

- inform your supervising social worker of any change in who lives in your home or any intention to move house

- keep a diary of events related to the child

- tell your social worker about any illness or hospital treatment the child has

- ensure that any information about the child is kept confidential.

And here are some examples of what you can expect from your fostering agency:

- that they will provide advice, information and support to help you perform the role of foster carer effectively

- that they will provide training to help you to develop your skills and knowledge

- that they will make sure any personal information is kept confidential.

There are also some expectations in terms of what the agency will do before, during and after a child is placed with you, including:

- that they will provide essential information about the child and their family history

- that they will seek your views about the child's

progress and provide any help needed to prepare written reports for meetings.

Working with the fostering agency

As a foster carer you are part of a team of people working to make sure a child gets the best possible care in the short-term and to develop a plan for their long-term care needs.

Since you are the person who spends the most time with the child, your insight into how they're feeling, how they're behaving and how they react to certain events or activities will be invaluable to discussions about how they're doing and what the next steps might be for them.

As we saw in chapter eleven, this means you will need to keep a record of how the child is getting on, their behaviour, any incidents and how you dealt with them. It's a good idea to record things as soon as possible after the event when your memory is fresh.

You'll need to be rigorous about confidentiality which means storing information about the child in a secure way and not sending sensitive information over email etc.

You'll also take part in meetings about the child where you'll be encouraged to update the team on their progress and behaviour.

Key people you'll be working with

As part of the fostering agency team you'll work with a range of different people connected to the child in your care. These will include:

Your social worker (also known as a supervising social worker or link worker): their role is to support and guide you and to assess how you're getting on. They might, for instance, recommend additional training for you. Your social worker will be your first port of call with any queries or concerns. You'll need to notify them about anything significant with regard to the child such as medical issues, accidents or holiday plans. Your social worker will also carry out supervision meetings with you on a monthly basis. These are more formal sessions where you will discuss any issues with the placement.

The child's social worker: their role is to support the child in your care. They're likely to meet with you and the child regularly depending on the child's situation and needs. They'll have contact with the child's family and with any court proceedings that are taking place.

The child's family: as we've seen elsewhere, a key part of your role, in most cases, will be to help the child keep in contact with their family, whether that's face-to-face, by phone or letters. The frequency and type of contact will have been decided upon as part of the child's care plan, based on what is best for them. You'll be supported by your agency to make contact with the birth family as safe and enjoyable as possible.

Independent review officer (IRO): usually employed by the local council, the IRO's role is to objectively assess the quality of care the child is receiving – not just from you, but from everyone involved in their care. They will meet with you once a year to see how things are going and get your feedback on the support and help you've received from the agency.

Other foster carers: most fostering agencies have support groups or forums made up of foster carers. These groups meet regularly to provide support and help to each other as well as an opportunity to simply let off steam. They're a great place to be able to talk to experienced carers who, at one time or another, have probably been through the same issues as you.

Teachers: foster carers are encouraged to attend things like parents' evenings and school events on behalf of the child in their care, so you will meet the child's teachers. Most schools have a designated teacher or support person who is responsible for ensuring that all looked after children in the school are getting the support they need.

Other childcare professionals: some children will need the support of other professionals, e.g. a therapist. If this is the case, you'll meet practitioners from the Child and Adolescent Mental Health Services (CAMHS) or other appropriate professionals working in this area.

Training and development

Your personal development plan

Within six weeks of being approved as a foster carer, you and your supervising social worker will have produced your personal development plan. This will detail your skills and list all the training and learning activities that you will need to improve and increase your skills and knowledge. It will also outline any support that you require. This plan will be reviewed and updated annually.

Your portfolio

You will need to create a portfolio of all the important documentation relating to your role as a foster carer. It is both a convenient way of keeping everything together but will also be invaluable in providing evidence of your skills and experience. Your portfolio should include:

- Copies of your fostering agency's policies and procedures

- The agency's foster carer handbook

- A health and safety checklist

- Your training certificates and any trainers' comments

- Letters of thanks

- Annual review comments

- Relevant supervision notes

- Recordings of critical incidents

- Observations/witness statements

- Your personal development plan.

Pre-approval training

As we have seen already, during the assessment process

you will receive training to give you some of the skills and knowledge you'll need should you be approved as a foster carer.

Training once you're approved

During the first 12 months of your time as a foster carer there are some very specific training and development requirements to be completed, known as Training, Support and Development Standards for Foster Care (TSD).

These seven standards have been set out by the Government and every foster carer must complete a TSD workbook to evidence how they meet those standards. Your fostering agency must provide the training and support you'll need in order to develop your knowledge and understanding of these standards and how you can apply them to your role.

The standards are:

- Standard 1: Understand the principles and values essential for fostering children and young people

- Standard 2: Understand your role as a foster carer

- Standard 3: Understand health and safety, and healthy care

- Standard 4: Know how to communicate effectively

- Standard 5: Understand the development of children and young people

- Standard 6: Keep children and young people safe

from harm

- Standard 7: Develop yourself

Your supervising social worker will help you complete the workbook by identifying where you need specific training and where your own experiences of fostering so far can be used as evidence of meeting the requirements of each standard.

Ongoing training

Your fostering agency should provide you with plenty of opportunities to continue to learn and develop your skills. Many offer training in specific topics, like attachment or play therapy or managing challenging behaviour. All training certificates should be added to your portfolio and will contribute to your professional development as a foster carer.

If you want to get a professional qualification in the subject, the Open University runs a number of courses in this area (see www.open.ac.uk/choose/ou/foster for more details).

Professional development

There is a career path for foster carers to follow if they choose. Working your way up means you increase your skills and experience and levels of pay (see chapter fourteen).

Many fostering agencies operate a three-tiered system, as follows:

Band one: newly-approved carers

Band two: foster carers who have completed their TSD courses

Band three: foster carers who have either completed a Level 3 diploma for Children and Young People's Workforce or are able to demonstrate skills equivalent to having completed the diploma. Band three carers are likely to be caring for children with more complex needs.

Your review

A formal review will take place annually to ensure that the care you provide continues to be up to scratch and that the child continues to get the support they need. It's a good opportunity to discuss any issues or concerns you might have as well as celebrating any achievements.

Support

As well as being responsible for providing you with training and development opportunities, your fostering agency is also there to support you on a day-to-day basis. This doesn't mean all day, every day, but your supervising social worker will meet with you regularly and should be at the end of the phone should you need help in-between times. Some agencies also have an out-of-hours phoneline you can call if need be.

You should also be able to meet up with your fellow foster carers at support groups or forums where you can share problems, stresses and issues as well as things that have gone well.

Protecting the child from harm

As we've seen elsewhere, many children in care have experienced neglect or abuse in the past. Clearly, therefore, one of the key roles of the foster carer and the team they're part of, is to protect the child from suffering further harm.

Your fostering agency will have a policy on 'safe care' which is likely to include a code of conduct around discipline, training on how best to care for a child who has been abused and how to recognise signs of abuse. There will also be guidance on how your agency will deal with allegations against foster carers.

Allegations

An allegation is a complaint or accusation that a foster carer has mistreated a child in their care. An allegation might be made by a member of the child's birth family, another professional or the child themselves.

This can be very stressful for the foster carer but it's important to recognise that there are many reasons why a child might make an allegation. It may be a way for a vulnerable child to feel more in control of their lives, or because they've mistaken something innocent as something more threatening; a reminder, perhaps, of an experience they had in the past.

Preventing allegations

Your fostering agency will provide training and advice about how to minimise the risk of an allegation being made against you. This will include guidance on how to care for a child in such a way that you do not put yourself in a compromising position. You will be encouraged to keep a daily log of events and to establish clear rules for the behaviour in your home, not just for the child but the rest of your family too.

If an allegation is made

An allegation covers a wide range of issues and doesn't automatically imply child abuse. The ways in which it is dealt with will depend on the nature of the allegation. But because there have been examples of children being ill-treated by their foster carers it is clearly important that any allegation is taken seriously and thoroughly investigated.

An assessment will be made as to whether the child should be moved out of the foster home. If appropriate, a full investigation will be carried out.

Support through an investigation

There are independent organisations which provide support to foster carers facing an investigation into an allegation.

The Fostering Network provides guidance on coping with an allegation. Members can also get impartial advice by calling their helpline. FosterTalk is an advocacy service which offers guidance and support, legal advice and counselling. Details on both organisations can be found in the Helpful Resources section.

Remember:

- Foster care is a professional role. There are certain standards that need to be met and you will be supported by your fostering agency to achieve them.

- When you first start as a foster carer you will go through a formal induction to introduce you to the agency's policies and procedures.

- You will be working as part of a team and will be invited to contribute your insight to help the team develop and implement the child's care plan.

- You will be working with a number of other professionals such as social workers and teachers, as well as the child's family and other foster carers.

- You and your fostering agency will formulate a training and development plan for you to build up your skills and experience.

- The fostering agency will provide you with lots of support to help you in your role.

- Sometimes a child will make an allegation against a foster carer. If this happens, an investigation will take place. It can be a very difficult experience but there is support available.

14. Pay and self-employment

Most foster carers don't foster for the money they get paid. They do it because they know it's important and they want to help, to make a difference. But clearly, you do need to know whether you can afford to foster.

Foster carers are paid allowances to cover the cost of looking after a child as well as fees which reflect their skills and experience.

This chapter outlines what these allowances and fees are as well as what it means to be self-employed and the impact that has on tax and pensions.

Allowances and fees

Foster carers are paid an allowance for each child in their care. If they do not have a child placed with them then they will not receive this payment.

They may also receive a fee payment which is based on their skill and experience level. Again, in the main, this is only paid if they have a child living with them. Some agencies pay a retainer to cover those periods when a carer does not have any children placed with them.

Some carers receive a salary. This usually applies to carers providing specialist care for children with highly complex needs.

Allowances

The Government has outlined the minimum allowances a foster carer should receive to cover the costs of looking after a child such as food, clothing, outings, activities etc. Details of these can be found at www.gov.uk/foster-carers/help-with-the-cost-of-fostering.

You may also receive allowances to cover special events like Christmas, birthdays and holidays.

Fees

Most agencies also pay a fee above and beyond these rates. This tends to be related to your skills and experience. A newly-approved carer is likely to start at the lower end of the scale and as their skills and experience increase, the rate they receive will increase. This might also reflect the fact that they are looking after children with more challenging needs.

These fees will differ across different fostering agencies. You can often find details of the fee structure on agencies' websites or you may have to ask for this information.

Being self-employed

In the main, foster carers are self-employed. This means they are not employees of the fostering agency and are therefore responsible for their own tax and National Insurance contributions. This may well be your first experience of self-employment and the idea might feel a little intimidating. However special arrangements have been made to simplify things for foster carers and in fact, much of what you earn will be exempt from tax.

Firstly, you'll need to register as self-employed with Her Majesty's Revenue & Customs (HMRC). You can do this online at https://online.hmrc.gov.uk/shortforms/form/CWF1ST or by calling the Newly Self Employed Helpline on 0300 200 3504. You should do this as soon as possible after being approved as a foster carer.

You may be issued with a tax return by HMRC which you will need to complete even if no tax is payable. This can be done online or using paper forms.

If your only self-employed income is from foster care and you're exempt from tax (see below) it is unlikely you'll receive a tax return in future, unless your circumstances change. If you're not exempt or have other self-employment income or your circumstances change you must inform HMRC.

Tax

Foster carers are exempted from tax if their total fostering income does not exceed what's known as a 'qualifying amount.'

The qualifying amount is individual to your circumstances and is calculated based on two elements added together. These elements are:

* Your share of the fixed amount of £10,000. This is based on each household so is shared equally if there are two carers in the same household.

* An amount per week for each foster child (£200 a week for a child aged under 11 and £250 a week for a child aged 11 or over). Part of a week counts as a full week.

So if, for example, you are a single carer and you've looked after a fourteen year old for the whole year and an eight year old for ten weeks of the year, then your qualifying amount will be:

* Fixed amount = £10,000
* 14 year old (52 weeks x £250) = £13,000
* 8 year old (10 weeks x £200) = £2,000
* Total = £25,000

Therefore if the payment (allowances and fees) received from your fostering agency is less than £25,000 there is no tax to pay on your fostering income.

If the payment received from your agency is more than £25,000 then you can choose whether to pay tax using the profit method or the simplified method. You will need to complete a self-assessment tax return in either case.

The simplified method means subtracting the qualifying amount from the total amount earned and paying tax on what's left. So if you earned £30,000 your taxable income will be £5,000.

The profit method means subtracting all allowable expenses from the total earned. So if you've earned £30,000 and have £27,000 of allowable expenses your taxable income will be £3,000. The benefit of the profit method is if the allowable expenses are more than the qualifying amount then you will have less tax to pay but it does mean having to keep more records of expenditure than if you use the simplified method. Full details about qualifying care relief can be found at:

www.gov.uk/government/uploads/system/uploads/attach ment_data/file/406706/hs236.pdf

HMRC has also developed an online tool specifically for foster carers, available at:

www.hmrc.gov.uk/courses/syob2/fc/index.htm

Record-keeping

- Keep a record of receipts of payment from the fostering agency
- Keep a record of the number of weeks that you care for each child in the year. Any part of a week can be counted as a full week
- Keep a record of the date of birth of each child
- Keep your records for six years after the end of the tax year to which they relate.

National Insurance contributions

Self-employed people have to make national insurance contributions based on their income. For foster carers the calculation is based on the amount over the qualifying amount.

Tax credits

You are not able to claim child tax credit for any foster children you look after.

You may be entitled to claim Working Tax Credit provided that you or your partner are in 'qualifying paid work' for at least 16 hours a week if you have a child of your own, or 30 hours a week if you do not. Foster care is 'qualifying paid work'. For more details visit www.gov.uk/foster-carers/help-with-the-cost-of-fostering.

Pensions

Since 2010, foster carers have been able to build up qualifying years for the state pension through weekly National Insurance credits, received once you've been approved.

Remember:

- Fostering is a job and foster carers are paid an allowance to cover the costs of looking after a child as well as fees which reflect their skills and experience.

- In most cases foster carers only receive this income when they have a child placed with them.

- Minimum allowance rates have been set by the Government. What the fostering agency pays over this minimum level is up to them.

- Foster carers are, in the main, self-employed. You'll need to register as self-employed with HMRC and may need to complete a tax return if your income is above a 'qualifying amount.'

- The qualifying amount is calculated based on the ages of the children placed with you and the length of time they stayed with you during the tax year.

- Foster carers pay National Insurance contributions on income over the qualifying amount.

- Foster carers can build up National Insurance credits towards the state pension.

Deciding to foster

You picked up this book because you were thinking about fostering. Having read it are you ready to decide whether to become a foster carer?

Hopefully now:

- You know whether you meet the basic criteria

- You've thought about whether you have the skills and qualities a foster carer needs, such as patience, resilience and commitment

- You are prepared for what the application and assessment process has in store

- You've been inspired by the experiences of the foster carers in this book

- You feel reassured that you will be trained and supported as a foster carer

- You've had many of your questions answered

- You know where to go to find out more

- You are excited about taking the next step.

Remember, every foster carer working today was once in the same position as you.

They were trying to decide whether to go for it or not. Worrying about how their family would cope. Unsure about what to expect. But they decided to go ahead and now are making an incredible difference to thousands of children every day.

Remember that fostering is an incredibly important and valuable role.

It provides a home and family life for some of the most vulnerable children in our society. It does so at a critical time in their lives, when the foundations are being laid for how they will develop as adults. These children deserve as normal a family life as possible. This is what foster carers are there to provide.

Remember that fostering is extraordinarily complex and challenging.

You don't need any special qualifications or education to foster. You don't need to have grown up in a 'perfect' family, or have raised 'perfect' kids. But you do need grit and determination to stay the course when times get tough. These children have been let down in the past and are likely to have developed some emotional and behavioural problems as a result. Problems you will have to deal with. But even when it feels like you're not getting anywhere, like you're banging your head against a brick wall, the very fact that you're prepared to stick at it will make an incredible difference to the life of your foster child.

Remember that fostering is uniquely rewarding.

Your patience, time and commitment will be rewarded. Every little step your foster child takes, like giving you a hug (Claire's story), a wave (Natalie's story), or slamming a door (Adele's story), is a sign of how your support is helping your foster child. These steps may not seem like much, but when they happen they feel like a really big, really heart-warming deal. What other job gives you the opportunity to make such an important and positive impact on a child's life?

Nearly 9,000 more foster carers are needed in the UK. Will you be one of them?

Good luck!

Quick answers to difficult questions

We all have questions we might be afraid to ask. Here are some common (but difficult to ask) questions and some quick answers. More detail is provided elsewhere in the book.

I want to foster but my partner/children aren't keen? Can I still go ahead?

In short, no. Fostering involves the whole family and requires everyone to be onboard. One of the tasks the fostering agency will undertake when you first make contact with them about fostering will be to explore everyone's position on the subject.

However, all is not lost. Many fostering agencies run information sessions that can be a really useful insight into fostering that might help your family feel more confident about doing it. Most run sessions for the children of foster carers too.

My partner has a criminal record from when they were young. Will this affect our application?

Not necessarily. It will depend on the severity of the crime and whether the offence was committed against children. The best thing to do is to discuss it with the fostering agency at the earliest opportunity to get their perspective on whether it might disqualify you from applying.

I've heard the application process is very intrusive. Why?

To protect the child who might be placed with the foster carer. The way in which applicants are assessed has been established to try and identify anything about the applicant that might reveal that they pose a risk to a child. Not all of that information can be gathered from the applicant themselves which is why a number of references and statutory checks are required.

Can I choose which child I foster?

As part of the assessment process you will agree with your fostering agency what age range and number of children you would prefer (and are best suited to) foster.

When a child needs a placement, the fostering agency will determine which of its foster carers can best meet their needs. This is called matching. They will discuss the child and their needs with you before making the placement and you have the option to refuse to take the child if you feel that's the right decision.

How much information about the child and their situation is given to the foster carers?

As much as is available. The foster carer is part of the team working to provide the best possible care for the child and therefore should have access to the same information as the rest of the team. This information can be invaluable in working out the particular issues that child has and how that might be manifested in their behaviour.

You will need to handle this information sensitively and keep it confidential.

What happens if a child doesn't like me?

Put simply, don't take it personally. Many people worry about this aspect of fostering so you're not alone. The important thing is to try and focus on why a child might be responding to you in a way that suggests they don't like you or don't like living in your home.

It could be the only means they have to express their fear about whether they're worthy of your care. It might be an attempt to protect themselves from you rejecting them.

In these circumstances, you'll need to try and put your own feelings of hurt and rejection to one side and work to help the child deal with their own, often very similar emotions. There's more on this in chapter eleven.

What sort of behaviour might I have to deal with?

All sorts. A foster child may behave in very challenging and sometimes inappropriate ways for their age. Much of this behaviour is the external display of many complex and, for the child, frightening and inexpressible feelings.

Your role is to deal with this behaviour in a consistent and supportive way and help the child to identify the feelings that underlie the behaviour and help them work out how to cope with these feelings. See chapter eleven for more on this.

How much contact will I have with the child's family?

As much as the child needs. It might be something you feel uncomfortable with, but it's really important for the child to be able to maintain and build their relationship with members of their family. The type of contact will be determined by the social work team and your role will be to support the child before, during and after any contact. See chapter eleven for more on this.

What if I can't cope?

It's natural to worry that you won't be able to cope with whatever fostering throws at you when you don't have experience of what that might be.

Firstly, remember that you won't be approved as a foster

carer unless the fostering agency believes that you can cope. That's what the rigorous assessment process is for – to discover your strengths and weaknesses, where you need more help and what type of fostering you're best suited for. You'll also receive lots of training to help build your knowledge, understanding and experience so that you feel much more confident.

Also bear in mind that you will have access to support, further training and the advice of other foster carers once you're approved – you will not be on your own.

However, having said all that, there will be days, weeks even, when you feel you aren't coping. When you want to throw in the towel and run for the hills. This is when you'll need to call on your reserves of resilience, patience and commitment and the support of your family and friends. You might even need to take a break.

Do we get paid?

Yes. Foster carers receive allowances to cover the costs of looking after a child and a fee that reflects their skills and experience. The Government has set out minimum rates for allowances which can be found at www.gov.uk/foster-carers/help-with-the-cost-of-fostering. There's more on this in chapter fourteen.

Glossary of useful terms

When you look further into the topic of fostering you'll come across a lot of technical jargon as well as familiar day-to-day terms that are used differently in this context. Here's a quick guide to some of these terms that you might find useful.

Adoption: a legal process whereby the guardianship of a child is transferred permanently from their birth parents to adoptive parents.

Allegation: when a child says that they have been harmed in some way by the people looking after them. An investigation will take place and depending on the severity of the allegation, a decision will be made as to whether the child should be removed from the carers' home.

Attachment: as soon as a child is born, they are programmed to form an emotional bond or 'attachment' with their main carer. Disruption to this bond through absence, inconsistent care or abuse can affect the child's emotional and psychological development which can be expressed through a range of behaviour, sometimes referred to as an 'attachment disorder.'

Beds: when a foster carer is approved, their approval will include the number of 'beds' they can offer. What this means is the number of children they have been approved to foster. This enables a fostering agency looking to place a child to quickly assess whether a particular foster family has capacity.

Birth parents / family: the child's biological parents / family.

Care order: when a child is taken into care because they are at risk of harm, the local council applies to the courts for a care order to take over day-to-day decision-making on behalf of that child.

Care plan: when a child is taken into the care of the local council, a team made up of a number of professionals will work together to develop a plan for that child's care. This will cover what type of foster care the child needs, what level of contact there should be with their family, any health or educational issues that need to be addressed, etc. The Government has set out standards for what should be included in a child's care plan.

Child protection register: this is a confidential list of all children in the local area who have been identified at a child protection conference as being at significant risk of harm.

Connected person care: (previously known as kinship care or friends & family care) this is when children on the child protection register are placed with other members of their own family, such as grandparents, aunts or uncles etc. These carers still go through an assessment process and have to be approved as that child's carers before the child is placed with them.

Contact: the formal arrangements agreed by the child's social work team for the child to keep in contact with their family. This will include what type of contact it is (face-to-face sessions, telephone calls, emails or letters), who the contact is with (not necessarily a parent) and how frequent the contact is (daily, weekly etc).

Corporate parent: this is the official term to describe the role of the local council towards the children in its care.

Friends & family care: see Connected person care.

Fostering: also known as foster care, this is when a child is placed with another family not connected with their own family. They will live in the foster carer's home for a short or long time until they either move back to live with their own family, are adopted or move onto other foster carers.

IFPs: previously referred to as independent fostering agencies/IFAs, these are independent fostering providers – organisations that recruit, train and support foster carers and provide their services to the local council.

Looked after children: this is one of the formal terms used to describe children who have been taken into care by the local council. The council assumes guardianship of these children and is responsible for finding them a suitable place to live for as long as they need it.

Matching: the process by which a child is placed with foster carers or adoptive parents. All aspects of that child's background, situation, physical and emotional needs are reviewed against details of a range of foster carers to make sure the child is placed with the carers who can best meet their needs.

Placement: the term used to describe when a child goes to live with their foster carers.

Safeguarding: everyone who works with children has a legal responsibility to make sure they are safe. Safeguarding policies, systems and procedures have been set up to enable individuals and organisations to do this as effectively as possible. Foster carers will receive training and support about how best to safeguard the children in their care.

Serious case review: a serious case review takes place when a child in the local council's care has been seriously harmed or if those organisations charged with keeping children safe have failed in some way and a child has been seriously harmed as a result. The review assesses all the evidence surrounding the case and makes recommendations for improvements in the way services are provided to try and avoid a repeat of any failings in the future.

Special guardianship order (SGO): foster carers can apply for a special guardianship order which is a formal court order giving parental responsibility for a child to someone else, in addition to the birth parents. This means the child will stay with the foster carer for the rest of their childhood, without being legally separated from their own parents.

Helpful resources

Websites

www.baaf.org.uk - British Association of Adoption and Fostering (BAAF) is a membership organisation for individuals and agencies working in fostering and adoption services. Visit the website for lots of advice and support and to find out about fostering agencies near you.

www.fostering.net - The Fostering Network is the UK's leading charity for fostering. On this site you'll find advice and support on all things fostering related including useful publications as well as community forums where foster carers discuss a wide range of issues.

www.fostertalk.org - FosterTalk is a not-for-profit organisation which provides support to foster carers on issues like tax and benefits and coping with allegations.

www.gov.uk - Search for 'fostering' to view Government policy, fostering regulations and national minimum standards as well as basic information about tax, pensions and how to apply.

Details of the relevant legislation and standards for Wales can be found at:

www.fostering.net/wales/legislation

Details of the relevant legislation and standards for Scotland can be found at:

www.fostering.net/scotland/legislation

Details of the relevant legislation and standards for Northern Ireland can be found at:

www.fostering.net/northern-ireland/legislation

Inspection reports

To find inspection reports for any fostering agency visit:

www.ofsted.gov.uk - England

www.cssiw.org.uk - Wales

www.scswis.com - Scotland

www.dhsspsni.gov.uk - Northern Ireland

www.hmrc.gov.uk - The main website for Her Majesty's Revenue & Customs (HMRC). You can use this website to complete your tax return online if you need to.

For more detailed information about self-employment, tax and fostering, visit:

www.gov.uk/foster-carers/help-with-the-cost-of-fostering and www.hmrc.gov.uk/courses/syob2/fc/index.htm

Book List

Attachment handbook for foster care and adoption

By Gillian Schofield and Mary Beek, BAAF, London, 2006.

A comprehensive exploration of attachment and how poor care in early childhood impacts on the emotional and behavioural development of children. It's detailed and, in places, a little technical but also includes lots of practical tips for how to care for children with attachment disorders alongside real life examples from children and their carers.

'If you don't stick with me, who will?' The challenges and rewards of foster care

Edited by Henrietta Bond, BAAF, London, 2005

A collection of first-hand accounts from foster carers about the realities of looking after foster children.

About the author

Emma Harding has spent much of the last 15 years helping people to understand what fostering is all about. Working with fostering services across the country, she's delivered many successful marketing campaigns to promote fostering and encourage people to think about becoming foster carers.

"*Foster carers are amazing people,*" says Emma, a freelance writer and project manager. "*The challenges they face are as diverse as the children they care for but they are all united in wanting to make a real difference to children's lives. I hope this book helps people to decide that they could foster so that more vulnerable children get the support they need.*"

For more information about Emma and her work, visit www.hilltopfostering.co.uk. You can also follow her on Twitter @emma_hilltop

19762632R00086

Printed in Poland
by Amazon Fulfillment
Poland Sp. z o.o., Wrocław